J. M. Coetzee

T0374999

J. M. Coetzee

*South Africa
and the Politics
of Writing*

David Attwell

UNIVERSITY OF CALIFORNIA PRESS
Berkeley • Los Angeles • Oxford

DAVID PHILIP
Cape Town • Johannesburg

University of California Press
Berkeley and Los Angeles, California

University of California Press, Ltd.
Oxford, England

© 1993 by
The Regents of the University of California

Published in southern Africa by David Philip (Pty) Ltd.,
208 Werdmuller Centre, Claremont 7700, South Africa
(ISBN 0-86486-247-4)

Library of Congress Cataloging-in-Publication Data

Attwell, David.
    J.M. Coetzee : South Africa and the politics of writing / David
Attwell.
    p.   cm.—(Perspectives on Southern Africa ; 48)
    Includes bibliographical references and index.
    ISBN 0-520-07810-1 (alk. paper).—ISBN 0-520-07812-8 (pbk. : alk.
paper)

    1. Coetzee, J. M., 1940– Criticism and interpretation.   2. Politics
and literature—South Africa—History—20th century.   3. South Africa in literature.   4. South Africa—History—1961   I. Title.
II. Series.

PR9369.3.C58Z635   1993
823—dc20   92-13468
                                                             CIP

Printed in the United States of America

An earlier version of chapter 1 appeared as "Contexts" in *Poetics
Today* 11:3 (copyright Duke University Press 1990). Part of chapter
2 appeared under the same title in *Novel: A Forum of Fiction* 25
(copyright Novel Corp. 1991). Reprinted by permission.

Quotations from *Dusklands, In the Heart of the Country, Waiting for
the Barbarians, Life and Times of Michael K, Foe,* and *Age of Iron*
are reprinted by permission of Martin Secker and Warburg Limited.
The author thanks J. M. Coetzee, Random House, and Viking for the
use of quoted material from other works by J. M. Coetzee.

For Joan and Kate

Contents

Acknowledgments

A number of people helped me to bring this work to a point where I felt I ought, finally, to leave it alone. My thanks go first to Bernth Lindfors, who was extraordinarily generous and loyal during my studies at the University of Texas at Austin. It is indeed a privilege to belong to that special category of disoriented colonials whose lives have been stabilized through Bernth's influence. My thanks go also to Barbara Harlow, whose questioning of my politics was a constructive inducement for me to clarify and deepen my arguments. Warm thanks are also due to Jack Farrell, Jaqueline Henkel, and Ramon Saldívar, all in Austin, Texas.

I would like to thank the Institute for Research Development and the University of the Western Cape for providing financial assistance in the form of grants and study leave. (The opinions expressed in this study are my own, of course, and are not to be attributed to these institutions.)

I owe a heavy debt of gratitude to the following friends and acquaintances in or from South Africa who took time to read early drafts, share my obsessions, and generally provide good counsel: Derek Attridge, David Bunn, Stephen Clingman, Brenda Cooper, Michael Green, Peter Kohler, Neil Lazarus, Tony Morphet, Benita Parry, David Schalkwyk, and Wendy Woodward.

Last, I must record my indebtedness to my family, Joan and Kate, for their tolerance of my neglect and neurosis, not to mention their willingness to undergo four intercontinental relocations in five years.

I am not a herald of community or anything else, as you correctly recognize. I am someone who has intimations of freedom (as every chained prisoner has) and constructs representations—which are shadows themselves—of people slipping their chains and turning their faces to the light.

J. M. Coetzee, *Doubling the Point*

Introduction

J. M. Coetzee's first six novels constitute a form of postmodern metafiction that declines the cult of the merely relativist and artful. Coetzee has absorbed the lessons of modern linguistics—the textual turn in structuralism and poststructuralism—yet seriously addresses the ethical and political stresses of living in, and with, a particular historical locale, that of contemporary South Africa. This book is an account of that achievement.

Despite the acclaim that Coetzee has received, both in South Africa and outside it, his fiction has been slow to attract sustained critical attention.[1] This is as true in South Africa as it is elsewhere: in South Africa the sheer power of the novels and—to an ear trained in the comfortable anglophone and positivist conversation of the South African liberal tradition—the strangeness of their idiom seem to have warned away many commentators, certainly those of Coetzee's own generation. A change came in the early to mid-1980s, when a number of essays established a certain consensus on the Left. Although it was by no means watertight, it held that Coetzee was a philosophical idealist whose fiction graphically portrayed the breakup of the dominating, rationalist subject of colonialism but who offered—depending on where the argument was grounded—neither an analysis of the play of historical forces nor a moral anchor in the search for a humane response to colonialism and apartheid.[2]

In 1988 the first full-length study appeared, Teresa Dovey's *The Novels of J. M. Coetzee: Lacanian Allegories.*[3] Dovey made it possible to speak properly of a critical debate; she challenged previous readings in a strongly theoretical discourse that showed, among other things, that the charges brought against Coetzee were blind to the strategies employed in the novels, and in particular that the parodic, allegorical, and deconstructive tendencies of the fiction had never been adequately recognized. In her relocation of the novels in a field designated "criticism-as-fiction, or fiction-as-criticism" (9), Dovey was able to make the startling but justifiable claim that the novels possessed a preemptive theoretical sophistication that disarmed the critics in advance. After Dovey's intervention it is no longer possible to ignore the novels' discursive complexity and self-consciousness.

Incisive as Dovey's critique was, it was also the victim of its own strengths, for in arguing against a naively referential view of novelistic discourse, Dovey seems to have erred on the other extreme. In her study Coetzee's novels are allegories of Lacanian theory, illustrations of a universalizing discourse on the self and its residence within language. If, as Coetzee objected in an address at a book fair in Cape Town in 1987, historicist criticism turns fiction into a "supplement" to the discourse of history ("The Novel Today" 2), then Dovey's theoretical allegory turns Coetzee's novels into a supplement to Lacan. Although Dovey does attend to the specificities of the South African context, she does so mainly in order to argue that, unlike Coetzee's novels, the discourses from the South African literary traditions that Coetzee parodies are unaware of their discursive conditions of possibility.[4]

Since Dovey's study, a number of essays have taken up her implicit call to postmodernist and poststructuralist theory, with the consequence that we now have a considerably oversimplified polarization between, on the one hand, those registering the claims of political resistance and historical representation (who argue that Coetzee has little to offer) and, on the other, those responsive to postmodernism and poststructuralism, to whom Coetzee, most notably in *Foe*, seems to have much to provide.[5]

However, as Dovey herself later pointed out, such polarization is false, for "it overlooks the potential area between the two, which is concerned to theorize the ways in which discourses emerging from diverse contexts, and exhibiting different formal assumptions, may produce *different* forms of historical engagement" ("Introduction" 5). I share this point of view. Indeed, one of the major premises of this study is that Coetzee's novels are located in the nexus of history and text; that is, they explore the *tension* between these polarities. As a novelist and linguist with a European heritage, working on the experimental fringes of his genre, Coetzee leans toward a reflexive examination of the constitutive role of language in placing the subject within history; yet as a South African, and one who returned to the country after a prolonged but finally unsuccessful attempt to emigrate, Coetzee cannot avoid having to deal with his national situation. Every attempt in the novels to hold South Africa at arm's length, by means of strategically nonspecific settings or socially improbable protagonists, simply confirms the intensity and necessity of this struggle. In the chapter that follows, I look into various forms of the relationship between *reflexivity* and *historicity*, examining these categories, as far as possible, within the South African situation. My critical apparatus entails a description of Coetzee's oeuvre as a form of situational metafiction, with a particular relation to the cultural and political discourses of South Africa in the 1970s and 1980s.

Although Coetzee respects the claims of both reflexivity and historicity, he does not seek a mediating or neutral role in the field of cultural politics. Behind the narrative subjects of each of the novels, behind Eugene Dawn, Jacobus Coetzee, Magda, the Magistrate, the Medical Officer, Susan Barton, and Elizabeth Curren, lies an implied narrator who shifts stance with and against the play of forces in South African culture. In other words, Coetzee's figuring of the tension between text and history is itself a historical act, one that must be read back into the discourses of South Africa where one can discern its illuminating power. We might call this narrator the self-of-writing, or the "one-who-writes," as Coetzee himself puts it ("Note on Writing" 42). Edward Said speaks of the "worldliness" of texts, which have "ways of existing that even in their most rarefied form are always enmeshed in circumstance, time, place, and society—in short, they are in the world, and hence worldly" ("The World" 35). This is no less true of Coetzee's novels; however, I would draw attention to the question of *agency* within this broader concept of worldliness. In South Africa a writer's worldliness expresses itself within a fragmented national context in which *positionality* is always at issue; thus, certain questions continually resurface: Who is the self-of-writing? What is his or her power, representativeness, legitimacy, and authority? (It is logical that the problem of agency, as defined here, should be so prominent a feature of white South African writing, yet no writer has examined the question quite as rigorously as Coetzee has done.) In the story told in this study, the movement of agency in Coetzee can be traced schematically: beginning with intervention and subversion

(*Dusklands* and *In the Heart of the Country*), agency passes through a moment of displacement, in the realization of its association with colonialism (*Waiting for the Barbarians*); it then finds a limited freedom in the moment-by-moment enunciations of textuality (*Life and Times of Michael K*) before ending in abnegation (*Foe*). In Coetzee's most recent novel, *Age of Iron*, there is a certain recovery of agency, but it is qualified in particularly somber terms.

The question of agency is linked to that of canonicity. It has often been remarked that Coetzee writes within a Western European tradition. This is a simple fact of his intellectual biography, a consequence not only of the global distribution of culture under colonialism but also of Coetzee's turning—like thousands of other South Africans before and after him—to the metropolis of Western culture for a better life and further education—hence his employment as a computer programmer in England, his studies in linguistics and stylistics at the University of Texas at Austin, and his subsequent appointment as professor of literature at the State University of New York at Buffalo. With this background Coetzee returned to South Africa in 1971 and began publishing fiction that not only draws on the European heritage—in particular, on novelists of high modernism and early postmodernism, notably Kafka, Beckett, Nabokov, and Robbe-Grillet—but that also continues to participate in some of the major intellectual currents of the West from the 1960s to the present, from the Chomskyan revolution in linguistics to Continental structuralism and, finally, to poststructuralism. It is perhaps too easily forgotten now that in the early to mid-1970s certain Western intellectual discourses offered to South Africans the possibility of cogent and liberating critiques of local conditions. For this reason the following chapter ends with a brief description of this moment in South African intellectual life and of the place of *Dusklands* within it.

In South Africa, however, Coetzee writes not as a citizen of the First World but of the Third—or perhaps the First within the Third—and therefore, like other white South African writers, he faces the problem of cultural authority. Bluntly put, his relationship with the European canon entails an accusation of complicity in a history of domination. Coetzee's response to this situation is to interrogate the specific form of marginality he represents. Although it is true that his novels are nourished by their relationship with canonical Western literature, it is equally true that through his complicated postcoloniality he brings that situation to light and finds fictional forms wherein it can be objectified, named, and questioned. As Derek Attridge correctly puts it, speaking of *Foe*:

> A mode of fiction that exposes the ideological basis of canonization, that draws attention to its own relation to the existing canon, that thematizes the role of race, class, and gender in the processes of cultural acceptance and exclusion, and that, while speaking from a marginal location, addresses the question of marginality—such a mode of fiction would have to be seen as engaged in an attempt to break the silence in which so many are caught, even if it does so by literary means that have traditionally been celebrated as characterizing canonic art. (217)

In *Foe*, Friday's enforced silence represents what a monocultural, metropolitan discourse cannot hear; but the silence also overwhelms and closes the novel itself, in an act of authorial deference on Coetzee's part. Friday's silence is therefore not only the mark of Coetzee's unwillingness to receive the canon as the natural breath of life; it is also the mark of history, and the mark of South Africa, in the text of a novel that scrupulously acknowledges its own limited authority.

This study addresses the developmental features of Coetzee's writing. *Dusklands* and *In the Heart of the Country* are paired as the early fiction; *Life and Times of Michael K* and *Foe* as the later. *Waiting for the Barbarians* is treated as the pivotal text in the corpus as it currently stands. Broadly speaking, the early fiction constitutes an attack on the rationalist, dominating self of colonialism and imperialism. In *Dusklands* the critique involves a bitter parody of scientific objectivity, of positivist historical discourses and narratives of exploration; *In the Heart of the Country* examines the ontological consequences of settler-colonialism's lack of social reciprocity. Both early novels make use of a teleology of decolonization to frame their critiques: by extension, *Waiting for the Barbarians* deals with the moment of the end, presenting a state of frozen anticipation that both subverts the semiotic supports of Empire and undermines the transcendental subject of History. *Barbarians* also begins the process whereby the limitations of white South African authorship are dramatized, though this dramatization is developed fully only in the later fiction, where Coetzee deals with the situation of writing in South Africa, writing, that is, in a crisis of authority. The logic of this development, from the semiotic emphasis of *Waiting for the Barbarians*, is plain: whereas *Life and Times of Michael K* explores the freedom of textuality, or of textualizing, *Foe* examines the conditions governing this freedom by historicizing them within the discursive conditions obtaining in South Africa—what I call its state of colonial postcolonialism. I conclude with a brief discussion of *Age of Iron*, which is both a summation of these trends and a departure from them. Coetzee seems to have won through to a position of being explicit about South Africa and its obsessions, more so, it seems, than at any earlier stage of his career; yet *Age of Iron* is also about death, about writing through and after death: we receive Elizabeth Curren's narrative of South Africa only once she herself has perished in her own, and the nation's, age of iron.

The "history" recovered here is partly the store of primary texts against which Coetzee positions his novels. It is made up of key discourses produced by colonialism and apartheid: the early fiction parodies "frontier" narratives, pioneer histories, and colonial pastoralism; at the midpoint of the oeuvre the historical text becomes the discourse of the apartheid state in its definitive moment of paranoia, that of "total strategy"; in the later fiction, although there is an ironic nod to another version of apartheid in the notion of "multinationalism," the primary texts are provided by the overwhelmingly politicized nature of South African culture—a kind of predatory hermeneutics—and, finally, by colonial storytelling, in the form of one of its founding narratives and its prototype, *Robinson Crusoe*.

In these readings I make selective forays into relevant areas of literary theory and draw, wherever appropriate, from Coetzee's own nonfictional writings in stylistics, metropolitan and South African literary criticism, political journalism, interviews, and essays and reviews on popular culture. Readers who have become accustomed to the notion that Coetzee's fiction represents a form of allegorized theory will find here a different emphasis; although he does borrow liberally from theoretical sources, the influences on his work are as often, and sometimes more decisively, literary rather than strictly theoretical. The essays in stylistics and criticism provide especially useful keys to understanding these influences. Dovey is correct to say that "with a writer like Coetzee, personal biography does not, indeed, seem very important" ("Introduction" 12). The readings offered here are by no means exercises in biography or biographical criticism. I have taken account of the nonfictional writings so as to return to the novels with what, I hope, are useful insights, in a project that has the more limited goal of explication. I would, of course, be pleased if these readings did not traduce what appears of Coetzee's intellectual biography on the surface of his writings; this seems to be a question of good faith, of being attentive to the life produced in, and by, these texts.[6]

Is "good faith" such a simple matter, however? In its own self-scrutiny Coetzee's writing forces such questions on us (traducement, it seems to say, does not depend on conscious choices). But my deeper misgivings in this study are more specific: for Coetzee to be the novelist that he is, he must pursue the path of fictionality; he is a specialist of the story and has declared his allegiance to this vocation without apology. Against this position—though, I trust, in ways that respect his versions of fictionality—I assert again and again the historicity of the act of storytelling, continually reading the novels back into their context. In this sense, I read Coetzee "against the grain." Uncertain, then, as to whether what I offer here is a tribute or a betrayal—infinitely wishing it to be the former—I turn to the theoretical and historical contexts brought into play by Coetzee's reflexive South African fictions.

ONE

Contexts: Literary, Historical, Intellectual

In January 1969, five years before publishing his first novel, Coetzee submitted to the University of Texas a stylistic analysis of the English fiction of Samuel Beckett. Toward the end of the dissertation he identifies in *Watt* two indications of Beckett's dissatisfaction with English, warning signs of his forthcoming decision to turn to French. They are "systematic parody" and "binary patterning at every level of language: words imitating the patterns of other words, and words setting up their own obsessive pattern" (also called "the rhythm of doubt"; 95, 163).[1] But having made these observations, Coetzee concludes his study with the following extraordinary paragraph:

> There is one further consideration we should not overlook if we wish to explain the nature of *Watt*. *Watt* was begun in 1941 and completed in draft in 1944. It is not entirely strange that during these years, while a statistician in Cambridge was copying *De imitatione Christi* word by word onto cards, while another statistician in a prisoner-of-war camp in Norway was tossing a coin and notating "H" or "I" [*sic*] one million times, that an Irishman in France should have been recording for posterity all the permutations which the nouns *door*, *window*, *fire*, and *bed* can undergo. ("English Fiction of Samuel Beckett" 164)

Coetzee does not refer to the fact that Beckett, when he was producing these permutations, was evading the Gestapo, living in Rousillon in the unoccupied Vaucluse. The reasons for Beckett's caution were his association with the French Resistance and the disappearance of his friend,

Alfred Péron (Kenner, *Samuel Beckett* 22). Coetzee is less interested in
such details than in the fact that Beckett was killing time as a prisoner of
the war itself, spinning out word games as a form of survival.[2] The
emphasis of Coetzee's observation, concentrating on Beckett's struggle
with history—a struggle encoded in prose narrative—is characteristic of
Coetzee's own work. In this view, narrative discourse is, without question, historically rooted—indeed, history is a tyrannical presence—but
more significantly, Coetzee is interested in the *consequences* of this
rootedness. If history is a determining and circumscribing force, the
question remains, what form of life is available to prose narrative as it
attempts to *negotiate* that determination and circumscription?

The problem is a large one, of course, far larger than Coetzee himself.
It touches not only on the complex and politically vexed question of the
textual turn in postmodern literary culture but also on the theoretical
conflicts between structuralism and poststructuralism, on the one hand,
and history or historical discourses, on the other. To examine the novels
of Coetzee contextually—that is, as novels both *about* and written *from
within* the South African situation—is to engage these larger issues. The
problem is complicated further by the fact that Coetzee admits to being
a linguist before being a writer and speaks of a creative relationship
between these functions.[3] In the era of structuralism's ascendancy in the
West, an intellectual allegiance such as Coetzee's involves far more than
simply being self-conscious about the nature of one's medium; it also
involves working into fiction nothing less than the notion that language
is a primary, constitutive element of consciousness and of culture at
large. However, through Coetzee's writing and its historical placement,
these modern Western intellectual currents flow into the turbulent
waters of colonialism and apartheid. The consequence is a fictional
oeuvre of unusual complexity, an oeuvre in which narrative discourse
and social conflict struggle for authority, in which ethical questions
fasten tenaciously to forms of reflexive play that elsewhere seem to have
made a virtue of relativism, and in which, finally, the West confronts the
limits of its own discursive powers, even its powers of subversion,
historicization, and displacement.

THE DEBATE ON REALISM

Coetzee cannot be confined to any particular tradition of linguistics or
linguistically informed literary theory. His brief memoir on his experience as a graduate student at Texas, his published notes on writing, and

his linguistic and critical essays reveal interests that include historical linguistics, generative grammar, stylistics, Continental structuralism and semiotics, translation (from Dutch, German, and Afrikaans to English), and deconstruction. The linguistic-systemic orientation of his novels involves the recognition, rooted in all linguistic inquiry, that language is productive, that "making sense of life inside a book is different from making sense of real life—not more difficult or less difficult, just different" (Coetzee, "Grubbing for the Ideological Implications" 4). This conviction, couched in broad terms here, has cost Coetzee a great deal in South Africa. Many writers, and many more readers, would see the assertion of that "difference" as a form of political and ethical evasion: in South Africa, life under apartheid seems to demand a realistic documentation of oppression. Both the white liberal tradition since Olive Schreiner, continuing down to the radicalism of Nadine Gordimer today, and contemporary black prose narrative since the era of *Drum* magazine in the 1950s have adopted various forms of realism as the unquestioned means of bearing witness to, and telling the truth about, South Africa.

The predominance of realism in South African literary culture has led Coetzee, when pressed, to adopt positions that waver between embattled defensiveness and incisive critique. The remark about life being different in a novel was made with reference to Sipho Sepamla's *A Ride on the Whirlwind* and Mongane Serote's *To Every Birth Its Blood*, in both of which Coetzee finds "a failure, almost a refusal [later, a 'programmatic refusal'] to create a structure in which there is some centre of intelligence." In the interview cited above, Coetzee traces the "refusal" to the continuing influence of European and American naturalism on the popular novel (4). I doubt that naturalism is really the source of the problem in this instance, since contemporary black prose narrative in South Africa owes much more to local traditions of journalism than to the Western popular novel. However, black writers themselves do not represent a homogeneous voice on this question, and some of them have held, and continue to hold, opinions that are in basic agreement with Coetzee's.

Coetzee is on record as having participated, at a very early stage, in a debate on the status of realism in black South African fiction, a debate started by Lewis Nkosi and taken up more recently by Njabulo Ndebele. Nkosi argued, in a famous statement of 1967, that black fiction was filled with "the journalistic fact parading outrageously as imaginative literature" and that seldom were "social facts" transmuted into "artisti-

cally persuasive works of fiction" ("Fiction by Black South Africans"
222). In 1984 Ndebele took up the theme, saying that a journalistic
documentation of oppression merely produces "an art of anticipated
surfaces rather than one of processes," "an art that is grounded in social
debasement," in which "little transformation in reader consciousness is
to be expected since the only reader faculty engaged is the faculty of
recognition. Recognition does not necessarily lead to transformation: it
simply confirms" ("Turkish Tales" 45).[4] Against "political exposition"
and the representation of oppression as "spectacle," Ndebele proposes
that writers begin to "rediscover the ordinary" by focusing on the details
of popular experience ("Rediscovery of the Ordinary" 143, 152).

Coetzee entered this line of argument by way of his essays on Alex La
Guma, the first of which, published in 1974, was written in response to
Nkosi. He begins by asking, "What value does the experimental line in
modern Western literature hold for Africa? . . . does not the Western
experimental line assume *and perpetuate* a rift between the writer and
society at large which is a fact of life in the West but need not become a
fact of life in Africa?" ("Alex La Guma" 6). The case of La Guma is
interesting, Coetzee shows, because it is experimental *without* falling
into the unwittingly conservative position adopted by Nkosi. In "Man's
Fate in the Novels of Alex La Guma" Coetzee goes on to argue, via
Georg Lukács's studies of realism, that La Guma is a critical realist who
politicizes his art by gesturing toward a revolutionary transformation of
history encoded in characterization and symbolism; thus, La Guma
arrives at narrative solutions that have an implicitly progressive social
hermeneutic. Coetzee's respect for La Guma and his grasp of realism's
epistemological limitations concur: in leaning toward social realism, La
Guma at least acknowledges a tradition, unlike the "refusal" that
Coetzee finds in the more recent prose of Sepamla and Serote. Since the
early 1970s Coetzee has followed other paths, but he has never abandoned this basic respect for the structural and political implications of
form.

There can be little doubt that South Africa's most accomplished
realist in the genre of prose narrative today is Nadine Gordimer. Not
surprisingly, therefore, Gordimer and Coetzee are frequently paired and
contrasted for their different approaches to fiction and its relationship to
society and history. It is possible, of course, to overstate these differences: Gordimer's "realism" often takes the form of a record of a
particular consciousness; moreover, in *The Conservationist*, as Stephen
Clingman rightly shows, she uses myth and symbolism to deliver a

critique that is as psychological as it is political (*Novels of Nadine Gordimer* 156–69). Nevertheless, Gordimer and Coetzee would seem to have fundamentally different views about the nature of narrative discourse. For Gordimer the essence of the writer's role lies in her social responsibility, and responsibility is treated primarily as a form of *witness*. Fiction will ultimately be tested by its accountability to the truth of its society, truth being the product of a dynamic interplay between what she calls "creative self-absorption and conscionable awareness" ("Essential Gesture" 298–300). To paraphrase, in terms of Gordimer's view one might say that narrative discourse *inhabits the writer*; it is the medium of her living connection to the social environment. Conversely, Coetzee might be taken to hold that the *writer inhabits narrative discourse*. Or to put this another way, when Roland Barthes speaks in *Writing Degree Zero* of "a corpus of prescriptions and habits common to all writers of a period," Gordimer takes this remark as a reference to the shared state of a language, from which writers depart in their individual ways ("Essential Gesture" 286); but in fact, Coetzee is much closer to the spirit of Barthes than is Gordimer, for he respects the limitations imposed by the inner structures of discourse. Coetzee's fiction could also be described as illustrating what Barthes elsewhere calls the shift in contemporary culture from *logos* to *lexis*, from knowledge to the word—categories that might be taken to mark the different emphases of the two writers in question ("Introduction" 114).

To argue that the writer "inhabits narrative discourse," however, is not to appeal to some ethereal realm above or beyond the social process, for Coetzee's position implies that narrative is itself a historical product, existing in tension with other discourses of the moment that are also the products of history and the bearers of culture. In terms of such a position, one will therefore ask not what is the proper self-definition of a writer but, rather, what forms of self-definition are *available* within the culture—available, that is, to the *writer*, whose relationship to society rests on the way in which he or she transmits the discourses of fiction.

FROM REPRESENTATION TO NARRATION

Coetzee is more concerned, then, with narrative and its relation to other discourses than he is with representation per se. However, just as Gordimer cannot be accused of being narrowly realist, neither can Coetzee be placed on one side of the theoretical conflict between textuality and historicity. Despite the discursive orientation of his fiction, it also establishes a historical narrative, one that is provided by the essential context of colonialism in each of Coetzee's novels. He has spoken about preferring "to see the South African situation [today] as only one manifestation of a wider historical situation to do with colonialism, late colonialism, neo-colonialism," adding, "I'm suspicious of lines of division between a European context and a South African context, because I think our experience remains largely colonial" (Coetzee, "Speaking" 23).

The basic narrative of Coetzee's oeuvre is indeed that of colonialism and decolonization. It underlies the entire corpus, which can be described sequentially as beginning with an aggressive imperialist violence in *Dusklands* followed by settlement of uncertain standing and duration in *In the Heart of the Country*. A defensive phase of anticipated revolution is presented in *Waiting for the Barbarians*, and in *Life and Times of Michael K* there is a stage of open civil warfare. *Foe* departs from the sequence but is no less concerned with questions of power and authority under colonialism, specifically, the power and authority of a mode of authorship straddling the metropolis and the colony, awaiting transformations that are as yet undetermined, perhaps indeterminable.

Up to and including *Michael K*, in other words, the fiction projects a teleology that pushes beyond the moment delivered up by the historical process itself. *Michael K*'s predictive admonition, in the form of a scenario of civil war, accounts for some of its critical energy; however, teleological conceptions of history are also questioned in the corpus. In *Waiting for the Barbarians* one finds a point at which history, in failing to transform the terms of discourse, becomes objectified as the myth of history, or History; with teleology thus undermined, the discursive nature of history is thrown into relief. This crucial and pivotal development enables Coetzee in his later fiction to explore the possibility that if history is not directly representable—if, as Fredric Jameson would say, our access to it is always textual (*Political Unconscious* 35)—then qualified forms of freedom might be discoverable in the *writing* of it. This marginal freedom, which is a function of textualizing, is staged in *Michael K* and later placed in question in *Foe*.

In hindsight one can see that Coetzee's struggle has always been to find appropriate points of entry into the narrative of colonialism for the specific interventions of which a self-consciously fictional discourse is capable. That this should have been and continues to be a struggle results from the general insistence in South African cultural politics that writers provide the solace of truth, of political faith, not fictive irritants, one might say, which leave readers with fewer defenses against the collective trauma they inhabit. Only recently has Coetzee begun to speak explicitly (and with some difficulty) of this struggle. In his *Weekly Mail* Book Week address of 1987 he demonstrates how sharply he feels the prevailing epistemological tensions: "In times of intense ideological pressure like the present, when the space in which the novel and history normally coexist like two cows on the same pasture, each minding its own business, is squeezed to almost nothing, the novel, it seems to me, has only two options: supplementarity or rivalry" ("Novel Today" 3). Being a *supplement* to the discourse of history, Coetzee goes on to say, would involve the novel in providing the reader "with vicarious first-hand experience of living in a certain historical time, embodying con-tending forces in contending characters and filling our experience with a certain density of observation" (3). *Rivalry* with historical discourse, by contrast, would lead to

> a novel that operates in terms of its own procedures and issues in its own conclusions, not one that operates in terms of the procedures of history and eventuates in conclusions that are checkable by history (as a child's school-work is checked by a schoolmistress). In particular I mean a novel that evolves its own paradigms and myths, in the process (and here is the point at which true rivalry, even enmity, perhaps enters the picture) perhaps going so far as to show up the mythic status of history—in other words, demytholo-gizing history. Can I be more specific? Yes: for example, a novel that is prepared to work itself out outside the terms of class conflict, race conflict, gender conflict or any of the other oppositions out of which history and the historical disciplines erect themselves. (I need hardly add that to claim the freedom to decline—or better, rethink—such oppositions as propertied/prop-ertyless, colonizer/colonized, masculine/feminine, and so forth, does not mean that one falls back automatically on moral oppositions, open or dis-guised, like good/bad, life-directed/death-directed, human/mechanical, and so forth.) ("Novel Today" 3)

Let me clarify why Coetzee should be so clinically articulate on this question. The polar opposite of Coetzee's position in the cultural politics of the period 1985–1987, the first two years of the States of Emergency and the years immediately preceding the address, would be the "People's Culture" campaign fostered by the United Democratic Front (UDF). (In the address Coetzee is talking about the politics of literature in reviewing and criticism, not about this particular campaign, but I refer to it as a prominent example of correct cultural activism in the period preceding Coetzee's remarks.) The campaign was not the first of the populist cultural movements of contemporary resistance in South Africa. In the late 1960s and 1970s Black Consciousness had a strong cultural program, one that was more coherent, in some ways, than that of the later movement. I shall return to Black Consciousness toward the end of this chapter; here, suffice it to say that Black Consciousness produced a central core of myths, a historiography, even a style that was distinctive. The poetry and fiction of Sepamla and Serote, as well as others such as Mafika Gwala, Mbulelo Mzamane, Mtutuzeli Matshoba, Ingoapele Madingoane, and a number of writers' groups publishing in *Staffrider* magazine, acquired a cohesive generational stamp, as cohesive as the work of the *Drum* writers of the 1950s. The more recent campaign, however, was less a system of self-affirming ideas than a set of socio-structural emphases, a way of conceiving cultural work as praxis, and it was linked to the resurgence of nonracial democratic or "Congress" nationalism in the 1980s.

Four features distinguished the People's Culture campaign: its concern with the accessibility of art to underclass audiences and readerships; its aim of building a "national culture" that would unite different oppressed groups under a common symbolic framework; its emphasis on a concrete, documentary form of realism that depicts the life experience of the oppressed; and, finally, its insistence that artists—"cultural workers"—submit themselves to the discipline of a formal alliance with the mass democratic movement (Press 36–37).[5]

It is easy to see why, in a literary environment significantly influenced by such priorities, the argument Coetzee makes for "rivalry" with the discourse of history involves him in a rather chilly political choice—a choice involving a refusal of association and consensus. These implications are spelled out without apology:

> I reiterate the elementary and rather obvious point I am making: that history is not reality; that history is a kind of discourse; that a novel is a kind of discourse, too, but a different kind of discourse; that, inevitably, in our culture, history will, with varying degrees of forcefulness, try to claim primacy, claim to be a master-form of discourse, just as, inevitably, people like myself will defend themselves by saying that history is nothing but a certain kind of story that people agree to tell each other—that, as Don Quixote argued so persuasively but in the end so vainly, the authority of history lies simply in the consensus it commands. . . . I see absolutely no reason why, even in the South Africa of the 1980's, we should agree to agree that things are otherwise. ("Novel Today" 4)

Coetzee does not share the seeming abandonment of deconstruction's *il n'y a pas de hors texte*; rather, the claim is closer to the Jamesonian idea that history is not available for direct representation. The risks involved in *making* this claim, however, are on the surface: the argument's authority rests in the fact that Coetzee knows exactly what he is up against.[6]

It is Coetzee's right to defend his position, of course, but there comes a point at which one wonders about the costs of such polemic, whether it obscures points of contact between the polarized extremes and, still more damagingly, obscures the forms of historicity that do, in fact, operate in Coetzee's own fiction. Against the drift of Coetzee's argument, therefore, I shall explore the relationship between history and fiction in theoretical terms that seem to be appropriate for the kind of fiction Coetzee's novels actually represent. I do so in the belief that if South African conditions produce what seems to be an impasse at the level of cultural polemic, it is reasonable to look outside the context for resources whereby the conflict can be reexamined.

SITUATIONAL METAFICTION

The problem now confronting us can be defined sharply: is the turn toward textuality in Coetzee a turning away from history? It is primarily, in other words, a question of *reference*. Hayden White describes this question as "the most vexed problem in modern (Western) literary criticism" (2n). It is not within the scope of this study to survey the problem in all its dimensions, but I shall touch on various theoretical models drawn from narrative theory and semiotics that enable us to place the conflict between fiction and history in broader perspective.

In Paul Ricoeur, first, we find a conception of what he calls "the narrative function" that succinctly shows the relation between "narrativity" and "historicity." Both elements, Ricoeur argues (following Wittgenstein), participate in the language game of narrating, the "activity" or "form of life" called "narrative discourse." The unity of these functions is evident in their mutual reliance on the notion of plot, which involves both "figure and sequence, configuration and succession" ("Narrative Function" 282–83). Their unity also exists in the fact that both forms of discourse incorporate reference "beyond" the surface of the text. In historical discourse, the existence of the referent is not questioned; in the case of fiction, reference is present, simply, in a qualified form: it is *"split or cleft reference,* by which I understand a way of relating to things which envelops, as a negative condition, the suspension of the referential claim of ordinary language" (293).

Ricoeur's formulation enables us to appreciate that even a posed, deliberate *suspension* of reference falls under the shadow of referentiality. This kind of speculation is developing among theorists of metafiction. Robert Scholes, for example, speaks of what he calls "modern fabulation" as a form of narrative that "tends away from direct representation of the surface of reality but returns toward actual human life by way of ethically controlled fantasy" (3).[7] In a more recent study that takes in the development of metafiction as part of its background, Robert Siegle argues that all narrative is reflexive to some extent and that where this function is in evidence, it draws attention to the conditions of meaning in a culture. Understood in these terms, reflexivity is a key element in what Siegle calls a "constitutive poetics" that is directed at "the mechanics and assumptions of composing, interpreting, structuring, positing," a poetics that is "a specialized application of a larger study of how a culture—whether in literature, cultural coding in general, science, or philosophy—composes its identity and that of its individuals and constitutes the 'world' within which it takes place" (11–12).

While drawing attention to the constitutive discourses of a culture, reflexive fiction also reminds readers of their own productivity. This position is outlined by Linda Hutcheon in *Narcissistic Narrative: The Metafictional Paradox*. In Hutcheon's view, metafiction has a foot in the door of its own interpretation, while only seeming to flaunt its independence from reality. In the conclusion to *Metafiction* Patricia Waugh asks the tougher question of "the politically 'radical' status of aesthetically 'radical' texts," a gesture that suggests implicitly that metafiction cannot escape historicization in the moment of its interpretation, even when its authors might prefer otherwise (148). Coetzee himself, recognizing that there are limits to the extent to which metafiction can determine its own historicization (in an argument I shall take up later in relation to *Michael K*), scrutinizes with some skepticism Vladimir Nabokov's implicit claims in *Pale Fire* to be able to preempt interpretation and assert the limitlessness of fictional mirroring ("Nabokov's *Pale Fire*" 4–7). Metafiction, then, in assuming the role of its own reader, merely foregrounds its complex and at times problematic relationship with history and society.

For Siegle, narrative reflexivity operates at a point at which "a thoroughgoing semiotics borders on ideological critique" (11). This remark can be substantiated by a brief examination of the historical themes developed by the Prague School in its extended inquiry into signification. Although the Prague School never formulated a theory of literary history or literature in history per se, F. W. Galan assembles one on its behalf in *Historic Structures*, showing it to have emerged implicitly in the course of the school's work over a twenty-year period. The stages in the development of the theory are as follows: (1) there was an attempt to resolve the apparent incompatibility between historical and structural linguistics, diachrony and synchrony, inherited from Saussure; (2) having reconciled structural linguistics with the phenomenon of linguistic change, the next step was to extend this approach to the question of literary evolution; (3) a conceptual and methodological break developed at this point from formalism to semiotics proper, after which the Prague School looked beyond literary immanence to the relationships between literary and other, social structures; (4) finally, attention was paid to the question of reception.

The stage that initially concerns us here is (3), at which point there was an attempt, largely by Jan Mukarovsky, to reengage the problem of signification from the point of view of its location *within the aesthetic function*. The position inherited from Jakobson was that the sign in literature is self-referential; consequently, it obstructs reference to reality. This position was reformulated to accommodate the insight that in order for the sign to operate *as a sign* within a communicative context, a referent must be present; the problem was therefore to understand the paradox between the autonomous and communicative features of the work. Mukarovsky resolved this paradox by showing that the literary sign had a special way of pointing to reality that preserves the specificity of the aesthetic function: its reference was oblique and metaphorical. But out of this observation comes the more significant and illuminating paradox: precisely because the referents of signs in poetic language have no existential value—since these signs are directed at nothing "distinctly determinable"—the literary work refers to "the total context of so-called social phenomena." It is because of this *global* quality of literature's reference to reality, involving a "unity of reference and intention" (Galan 116), that it provides valuable images of the texture of historical epochs. Later in the history of the Prague School, Mukarovsky incorporated the category of the subject into his description of signification. The position, as modified by this final move, is formulated by Galan as follows: "The reality which as a whole is reflected in the aesthetic sign is also unified in this sign in accordance with the image of the unified subject" (117).

In its theorization, then, of signification and the concretization of meaning in reception, the Prague School would seem to have anticipated the course of later commentaries on reflexive narrative. But to complete this excursus: from such threads of narrative and semiotic theory it appears that one could legitimately speak of a *situational metafiction*. This would be a mode of fiction that draws attention to the historicity of discourses, to the way subjects are positioned within and by them, and, finally, to the interpretive process, with its acts of contestation and appropriation. Of course, all these things have a regional and temporal specificity.[8]

POSTMODERNISM AND POSTCOLONIALISM

Any discussion of metafiction today must pay some attention to what has become known internationally as the postmodernism debate. This is essentially an argument over the political status of what Jean-François Lyotard calls postmodernism's "incredulity towards metanarratives" (xxiv). The argument I have conducted thus far, on the relationship between reflexivity and historicity, implicitly adopts a position in this debate, one that shares with Linda Hutcheon a certain regard for the "paradoxically worldly" condition of particular forms of postmodern writing (*Politics of Postmodernism* 2). My account of Coetzee's fiction, however, touches on the question of postmodernism only *in medias res*, for although Coetzee's oeuvre draws significantly on modernism and its legacy, its strength lies precisely in his ability to test its absorption in European traditions in the ethically and politically fraught arena of South Africa. The problem, in other words, is to understand Coetzee's postmodernism in the light of his postcoloniality.

Here we run immediately into difficulties with respect to the postmodernism debate because the cosmopolitanism of the debate has become an obstacle to understanding the unique features of postmodern literature in different regional contexts. How we theorize about postmodern literature produced on the periphery of colonialism must involve an interplay between metropolitan and nonmetropolitan sources, but the *specificity* of regional forms of postmodernism is vulnerable to misrepresentation in the international scene. (The postmodernism debate is perhaps itself an instance of the global, homogenizing spread of postmodernity, a process embodied, in this instance, in the academic book trade.) Neil Lazarus, in a valuable essay on contemporary white South African literature, illustrates this vulnerability. Lazarus applies Theodor Adorno's account of the critical potential of modernism to the writing of Gordimer, Coetzee, André Brink, and Breyten Breytenbach. In the course of argument the following point emerges:

> This literature must now be defined not only by its negativity, but also by its marginality and acute self-consciousness. And one is tempted to ask whether a literature displaying these characteristics, and written after—and frequently even in the idiom of—Kafka and Beckett and, for that matter, Kundera, could be anything other than modernist; especially when it is borne in mind that as a discourse it is so *ethically* saturated, so *humanistic* in its critique of the established order, so concerned to *represent* reality, and so *rationalistic* that it would be quite inappropriate to describe it as postmodernist. (148)

I share Lazarus's appreciation of the ethical value of this writing, but what is puzzling is his insistence that it would be impossible for postmodernism *in any form* to achieve an ethical stance; indeed, Lazarus drives the point home in a footnote, saying that he would "go so far as to argue . . . that 'postmodernist' literature in South Africa could only be reactionary" and that an aesthetic of modernism, because of its "rational humanism," "might well exist as the only aesthetic on the side of freedom" (148). But in the case of two of the writers mentioned—namely, Coetzee and Breytenbach (to a lesser extent Brink)—the label "modernist" does not explain the fact that these writers have relied on major developments in the European novel since the nouveau roman in developing their own responses to the state of deadened moral consciousness produced by South African oppression. If the decadence of postmodernism is assumed, then the oppositionality of white South African writing can be substantiated only by identifying it with earlier forms of modernism; but as we have seen, this maneuver entails an anachronism. What Lazarus says about white South African writing, via Adorno's aesthetic theory, ought to enable us to challenge the by now orthodox view of postmodernism, which is informed by the essentially metropolitan experience of post-1968 disillusionment, its accommodation to the postindustrial age, and its subsequent celebration of relativist experimentation. The fact that South Africa does not share this experience does not mean that postmodernist techniques do not percolate through its literary culture, taking on new forms and acquiring a different animating spirit.

In other words, there is postmodernism and there is postmodernism. In Australia and New Zealand, Simon During, Helen Tiffin, and Stephen Slemon have developed an interesting critical discussion of the specificities of postcolonial literary practices, partly in response to what they see as a lack of regional sensitivity within Euro-American versions of the postmodernism debate. Slemon argues, for instance, that a great deal of the work being done in the name of postmodern literary studies remains unaware of the historically "grounded" strategies of "de-essentialization" evident in postcolonial literatures; this ignorance of postcolonial literatures "is perhaps contributive to postmodernism's overwhelming tendency to present itself . . . as a crisis, a contradiction, an apotheosis of negativity" ("Modernism's Last Post" 14).

The unique contribution of these critics has been their attempt to clarify the *range* of situations and discursive strategies emerging in postcolonial literary cultures. During's point concerning what he calls the "crisis of emptiness" in "postcolonizing" (as opposed to "post-colonized") discourses is particularly relevant to the situation of white South African writing:

> The crisis of postcolonialism is not just a crisis for those who bore the burden of imperialism: who have seen the destruction of their modes of production, the de-privileging of their language and the mutilation of their culture. It is also a crisis for those who have been the agents of colonialism and who, once colonialism itself has lost its legitimacy, find themselves without strong ethical and ideological support. (370)

The challenge facing these writers, During argues, is to find a language that encodes new forms of historical and ethical vision *without* unwittingly celebrating colonialism's material and epistemic capture of the colonized world and its traditions. Tiffin speaks of a "canonical counter-discourse" that is characteristic of writers in this situation ("Post-Colonial Literatures and Counter-Discourse" 22); elsewhere, she argues that canonical counterdiscourse, like nationalist literatures in which the recovery of identity is a more or less feasible project, "still promotes polyphony, eschews fixity, monocentrism and closure, interrogates concepts such as history and textuality, opposes oral to written formulations, but does so by inhabiting the absences or the oppositional 'positions' in the imperial textual record, and from these absences or oppositions interrogating its presence or fixity" ("Post-Colonialism" 176). Coetzee's carefully positioned metafictional constructions would certainly fit this description. Slemon has distinguished the forms of reiteration such projects involve from those of the metropolitan postmodern strategies discussed by Hutcheon in her studies of metafiction; like metropolitan postmodernism, Slemon argues, postcolonialism involves a parodic repetition of dominant, imperial forms of textuality, but unlike it, postcolonialism—including its "postcolonizing" varieties—remains basically oppositional and retains a "referential" or "recuperative" relationship to national issues ("Modernism's Last Post" 7–9),

To continue the implicit direction of this discussion, one ought to make further distinctions with respect to South Africa (though Coetzee provides these scholars with several examples of their leading propositions), for it needs to be acknowledged that there are fewer grounds in South Africa for the degree of optimism evinced by Slemon concerning the critical capacities of "postcolonizing" literature. What During calls the "crisis of emptiness" remains a significant determinant of white South African writing, so that the limited, marginal option of consistently "eroding one's own biases," as Tiffin puts it ("Post-Colonial Literatures and Counter-Discourse" 32), emerges as an ethically appropriate strategy in the armory of the postcolonial writer. Coetzee has fine-tuned this strategy to the extent of making it a hallmark of his later fiction. The fact, however, that he has developed fictional forms that dramatize so acutely the limitations of their authority raises questions about Coetzee's national situation that need to be addressed in different terms.

THE POLITICS OF AGENCY

The problem of authority, which is sharply focused in Coetzee's fiction, forces us to raise new questions concerning his relationship with his social environment. This is difficult terrain, however, because finely contextualized readings have been heavily influenced in recent years by symptomatic critiques. But what would it mean to contextualize so self-conscious a mode of writing as Coetzee's? Can a "symptomatic" reading be imposed on what is *already* a symptomatically sensitive discourse? There is some danger here that discussion might devolve into a sterile series of assertions and counterassertions about the relative weight of the diagnoses being offered. Bearing this in mind, I follow a path that respects the fiction's own symptomatics but that simultaneously reads Coetzee's novels as historical products; to do so, I invoke the concept of *agency*.

First, a distinction is needed. The notion of agency referred to here is unrelated to the problem in Marxist hermeneutics of how agency is to be considered as a form of revolutionary discipline within a dialectical understanding of historical causality. Rather, it has to do with the concept of nationhood—itself a significant lacuna in Marxist theory— that is, with questions of inclusion and exclusion, of finding or not finding a place for one's own particular story within the framework of the broader, national narrative. Agency, in the context of a fragmented state of nationhood like South Africa's, therefore serves as an umbrella concept for such notions as *legitimacy, authority,* and *position.*

Literary-intellectual life in South Africa is as subject to the divisions within the national polity as any other kind of social activity. For example, Antonio Gramsci's distinction between organic and traditional intellectuals (3) has been widely popularized on the South African Left. These categories can no doubt be put to use in more disinterested ways, but their usefulness to South Africans is undoubtedly tied up with the fact that they have provided many intellectuals with the means to validate themselves and denounce others in a country in which the social distance between intellectual and popular sectors remains embarrassingly visible. Although class factors are, of course, in evidence within black intellectual circles as well, race is a crucial determinant, perhaps the final determinant, of the social composition of intellectual life. And although democratic nonracialism provides a set of core values to which it is possible to appeal, the structural constraints built into educational institutions, scholarly disciplines, and, to a lesser extent, literary practices are inescapable. The national situation, in other words, in which intellectuals and literary artists work imposes on them a politics of agency.[9]

In Gordimer one can see the problem fictionalized both in Rosa Burger and in Hillela in *A Sport of Nature,* where the central issues involve the positions these protagonists achieve within the emergent body politic. Gordimer also deals with the issue explicitly in her 1982 lecture "Living in the Interregnum":

> There is a segment preoccupied, in the interregnum, neither by plans to run away from nor merely by ways to survive physically and economically in the black state that is coming. I cannot give you numbers for this segment, but in measure of some sort of faith in the possibility of structuring society humanly, in the possession of skills and intellect to devote to this end, there is something to offer the future. *How* to offer it is our preoccupation. Since skills, technical and intellectual, can be bought in markets other than those of

the vanquished white power, although they are important as a commodity ready to hand, they do not constitute a claim on the future.
That claim rests on something else: how to offer *one's self*. (264)

Although this emphasis in Gordimer on the self's search for position in a newly emergent body politic is a poignant feature of her work, it is not always kindly received by others with an equal claim on the future. Lewis Nkosi, for example, says of *A Sport of Nature*, "A great part of the motivating force of this fiction is its fear of exclusion, the fear of loitering without intent in the vicinity of revolution" ("Resistance" 46).

Edward Said's concept of "worldliness," therefore, has an unhappily pertinent application to South Africa. In the case of the novel, the implied narrative subject—Coetzee's "self-of-writing"—resides within a web of dangerously consequential connections defined by relations of power in a society in contradictory stages of casting off the colonial yoke. Coetzee's narrative of colonialism has dramatized this situation implicitly in terms of rivaling nationalisms; in this respect, he has not shared the view of more strictly Marxist revisionists, for whom class struggle in the context of the industrial transformation of South Africa has been more significant than questions of race and nationhood have been. (In the early 1990s these elements seem to be "in solution" as never before: both radical and moderate nationalisms have begun to transcend racial divisions.)

By contrast, Coetzee's emphasis on race and colonialism seems to have been the result of biographical accident rather than the product of a desire for accurate historical representation. Although it is rarely acknowledged, Coetzee is in fact a regional writer *within* South Africa. His sense of the landscape and the history of the country has been shaped by his familiarity with the Cape and the Karoo, with their histories of slave and master-servant relations and "frontier" policies, rather than by the mining and industrial conditions of Johannesburg, conditions that make the Transvaal, by Coetzee's own admission, "practically a foreign country" to him ("Two Interviews" 458). The racial and colonial emphasis was reinforced later, of course, by the influence of the Vietnam War on Coetzee's thinking. Given this emphasis, Coetzee has been less inclined to invest in the notion of the self's finding a home within the future. Instead of Gordimer's leaps of faith, which have produced intriguing moments in her fiction—notably the ending of *July's People*, which continues to fuel critical discussion[10]—Coetzee provides the image of a wary, increasingly marginal narrative subject who deftly negotiates the interstices of power, maintaining its ethical integrity but avoiding not only appeals for inclusion but also any over-statement of its own legitimacy and authority. Moreover, instead of this process being undertaken by the existential or historical *self*, as Gordi-mer defines it, it is undertaken in Coetzee by the subject of *writing* and becomes an element in the efforts of the fiction to textualize its own conditions of possibility.

An uncompromising question, at this point, would be to ask whether, in his unusual sensitivity to the problem of marginality, Coetzee in fact represents no one but himself—after all, he is distinguished not only by a Cape-specific background but also by a degree of intellectualism unmatched by any other South African writer. One of the effects of his intellectualism is that his fiction tends to distill what are essentially *heuristic* models into narratological forms—as in Friday's speechless-ness, for instance—thus giving them a kind of ostensible "universality," a representativeness that they would lack were they written in a less refracted way.

But there is a powerful corollary to such a question: if Coetzee is more intellectual than many other writers, and also less obviously affiliated politically, then is he not more at liberty to articulate general conditions? This is not to suggest that he has superior insight, necessar-ily, but rather that his relative detachment enables him to be more explicit and more honest about his own social placement than more obviously engaged white writers can be about theirs. The question of audience affects every writer in South Africa, but Coetzee is unique in achieving a degree of critical objectification and control over the prob-lem. Such, then, is Coetzee's politics of agency. The novel that takes up this issue most clearly is, of course, *Foe*, which gets behind the self-of-writing and questions its self-representation by setting it before the figure of Friday, who anticipates the silent, transformative potency of the body of history, the body of the future.

COETZEE AND REVISIONISM

Thus far I have noted the differences separating Coetzee from certain streams of radical thought in South Africa. Now let me explore the similarities. The implications of a potentially revolutionary historical situation are present from the beginning of Coetzee's oeuvre; in this sense he participates in shaping a literary-intellectual moment that be-came generally understood as "postliberal." Thus, I shall explore the situation to which *Dusklands* contributed by placing Coetzee's entry into fiction writing alongside the key social debates that were taking place in the country at the time.

In the early to mid-1970s South Africa began to reap the whirlwind over apartheid. The period saw a number of developments that either heralded the possibility of major historical transformation or responded to such a possibility. The most important of these developments were the rise, during a severe recession, of a militant independent labour movement culminating in large-scale strikes in the Durban area in 1973; the increasing militancy of black students and the rise of Black Consciousness, which quickly became popularized in schools and local communities and played a decisive role in the Soweto Revolt of 1976; and, finally, beginning in 1977, the development of the strategy of "reform" by the state as an attempt to manage the crisis it was facing by refining the constitutional, administrative, and economic structures on which its hegemony was based.[11] From this period on, then, South Africa seemed locked into an opposing set of categories, "revolution" or "reform," both of which drew their defining features from the large-scale historical momentum with which the decade had begun (Stadler 161–84).

In this climate an academic revisionism dating from the late 1960s in the field of historiography acquired a particular urgency. The origins of the movement, as its influence and purview increased and widened to embrace all the social sciences and humanities, would have to be traced to the prominence of radical philosophies in Europe in the 1960s (mainly existentialism and structuralism and, on a lesser scale, Marxism) and to the antiwar and civil rights movements in the United States. In the local situation these powerful models of the metropolitan culture seemed to open up new vistas of consciousness and praxis in a South Africa seemingly deadened by apathy, acquiescence, and repression.

The exemplary book of the period was *The Eye of the Needle* (1972), and the exemplary life was that of its author, Richard Turner, who was assassinated in 1977. Turner's exposure to existentialism and Marxism while a student in Paris in the 1960s translated into the conviction, expressed in his life and work as a labor activist and lecturer in philosophy, that objective conditions in South Africa were the consequence of human choices and actions and could therefore be challenged. *The Eye of the Needle* was written specifically to popularize this concept and to project ethical and political alternatives as being thinkable in a culture that blocked them. Herbert Marcuse's *One Dimensional Man* is a high point of the period, with its resistance to "the closing of the universe of discourse" and its critique of the associations between Reason, techno- logical rationality, and domination (themes that echo in *Dusklands*). Turner gave currency to Marcuse, publishing an essay entitled "Marcuse: The Power of Negative Thinking" in the University of Cape Town student journal *Radical* (1970). Turner's most rigorous philosophical project, however, written while under a banning order, was an incom- plete and unpublished analysis of the problem of "the nature and status of the knowing subject in a materialist dialectic" (Morphet, "Introduc- tion" xxix). Apart from its obvious philosophical importance, the treatise's pertinence lay in its attempt to reconcile the different aspects of Turner's own life, to combine, in other words, a defensible ethical standpoint that was meaningful from the point of view of the subject with a firm grasp of the material forces underlying the larger, enveloping crisis (xxx).

The representative feature of Turner's life and work is this attempt to combine a particular perspective on the self with a larger, historical view. It is a problem toward which South Africa seems prone to drive its more thoughtful citizens. The prominence of autobiography since the early 1960s, in black writing especially, is evidence of this trend, but it is particularly visible in two major discursive events of the early 1970s: Black Consciousness itself and the Study Project on Christianity in Apartheid Society (SPRO-CAS). The Black Consciousness position was one of self-recovery and self-affirmation in response to the negations of racism. The black world was posited as an organic unity, a trans- individual mode of selfhood, and it was reinforced by a teleology of moral justice. The resources used by the early exponents of Black Consciousness were classic statements of black assertion such as Frantz Fanon's *The Wretched of the Earth* and Stokely Carmichael's *Black Power.*

SPRO-CAS was initiated by Beyers Naude in mid-1969 with the following objectives: "to examine our society in the light of Christian principles; to formulate long-term goals for an acceptable social order; and to consider how change towards such a social order might be accomplished" (SPRO-CAS 1). The project established six commissions to address issues in economics, education, law, politics, society, and the church. The ethical framework underlying the project was defined in terms of three principles: the "sanctity of the human person," the need for redemption and reconciliation, and the necessity of working "with our whole being now towards the maximum of justice and love in all human relationships" (5–6). The project combined the efforts of prominent white liberals from a range of backgrounds, but it also won participation from people like Turner as well as black intellectuals like Steve Biko and Ben Khoapa (who were spokespersons of Black Consciousness), Njabulo Ndebele, and, curiously enough, Gatsha Buthelezi. These two forms of critique, the most prominent of the period, were ragbags of critical thought articulated by people forming, in the case of SPRO-CAS, an unlikely alliance on the basis of a common opposition to apartheid.

The state took the challenge seriously, however. The Schlebusch Commission was set up to investigate the National Union of South African Students (NUSAS), the Christian Institute (closely linked to SPRO-CAS), and the Institute of Race Relations. Its report, published in 1974, is a compendium of the minutiae of the day-to-day affairs of these organizations and their representatives, not excluding their private lives. Its distortions of logic are usually banal, although the consequences in terms of bannings and restrictions were not. An example is the chapter "Polarisation," an account of the formation, under Biko's leadership, of the South African Students Organization (SASO); this chapter tries to show that because Black Consciousness incorporated a dialectical account of the progress from racism, to black assertion, to an ultimately nonracial future, its whole method and its ethnic emphasis were a mask for a Leninist dialectical materialism (Schlebusch Commission 391–463). On the cultural organization within NUSAS called Aquarius, the commission quotes reams of evidence from student leaders apparently proving their de facto guilt by stating that they objected to the environmental conditioning around them (334–52). In these examples and others the commission tries to pin down subversion to particular configurations of thought or consciousness: for all parties, it seems, including the state, undergoing "paradigm shift" became a quintessentially political act.[12]

In the academic context the initial focus of the historiographical debate was the two-volume *Oxford History of South Africa*, edited by Monica Wilson and Leonard Thompson. For the revisionists (represented by F. W. Johnstone, Stanley Trapido, Harold Wolpe, Colin Bundy, Martin Legassick, Shula Marks, and Charles van Onselen) the kind of history it represented implied a liberal-positivist conception of racial "interaction," a top-down sense of agents and actors that underplayed the role of the underclasses and of structural factors in determining events, and a gradualist or reformist perspective on change. Above all, however, the debate centered on how the relationship between capitalism and apartheid was to be examined. In the liberal view, apartheid was irrational, and the dynamics of growth in a free market system were bound to undermine steadily the ability of the state to enforce it. In the revisionist viewpoint, apartheid was intrinsic to the logic of capitalist accumulation because it provided, among other things, for cheap labor by such means as regulating urbanization through the pass laws. Whereas liberal history implied that capitalism was a progressive force acting on and transforming precapitalist cultures and social structures in preparation for their assimilation into the "developed" world, revisionism held that capitalism was an invasion linked internationally to imperialism and that the proper object of study was the capacity of underclass communities to resist this presence, or at least to transform it according to their own interests (Marks 166–69).

From an early stage a similar renarrativization of South African history penetrated the literary culture. The conference held at the University of Cape Town Summer School in 1974, whose proceedings were published under the title *Poetry South Africa*, was undoubtedly a watershed. In particular, in the debate between Guy Butler and Mike Kirkwood one discerns the clash of fundamentally opposed systems whose scope includes historiography, literary practice, and cultural identity and commitment. What Kirkwood challenged was not Butler himself so much as "Butlerism," a certain liberal sense of what it meant to be an English-speaking South African (an ESSA, in Butler's account). This perspective looked back to the arrival of the 1820 settlers in the spirit of mission, in that the historical role of the English was thought to be an enlightening, humanizing one in a "frontier" society of harshly contending forces and ideologies. For Butler, the English were "Athenians," "traffickers in ideas, and in the arts, transmitters and popularizers of ideas and new ways of feeling" (quoted in Kirkwood 103). As the bearers of the English language, the English had a role to play in education and in the literary arts, but the social dimensions of Butler's thinking embraced involvement in every sphere, including (constitutional) politics. The historical reality of the settlers' positioning in a "buffer zone" between warring Xhosas and Afrikaners was rewritten as a cultural and political program: the English were to be "mediators," facilitating the emergence of a more humane national culture and polity. The approach was essentially Arnoldian, *Culture and Anarchy* transposed from the class fractures of nineteenth-century England to the South African "frontier."

Kirkwood's challenge was based on a recontextualization of the ESSA identity in terms of imperialism. The historiographical aspect of the argument rejected the thesis that the English occupied a middle ground; the position occupied by the English was one they *shared* with the Afrikaners, namely that of the ruling class in an essentially colonial set of relationships, where stratification took on a racial coloring. Revisionist historiographers introduced the materialist argument into the terms of debate, and they are taken up by Kirkwood here; but Kirkwood goes on to examine the subject-position of the ESSA as colonizer, with reference mainly to Fanon's *The Wretched of the Earth* and Albert Memmi's *The Colonizer and the Colonized*. In a reading faithful to the informing philosophies of his sources, Kirkwood combines the materialist historiographical critique with the psychoanalytic and existentialist critique of imperialism. The heart of his presentation was to outline a three-part process whereby the "ontology of the colonizer" was revealed:

In the first [stage] there is an emphasis on cultures rather than on societies, on functional-structuralist anthropology, and on such matters as "the primitive mind." The characteristic of this phase is the confidence with which the colonizer makes the collective being of the colonized his object, fails to assert a critical awareness of his own ethnocentric assumptions and projections, and uses the colonized as exotic models for rudimentary raids into the fascinating history of his own psyche.

In the second an awareness of the colonial society as such is dawning but the colonizer retains the role of its interpreter. Mannoni's classic work, *Prospero and Caliban, the Psychology of Colonization*, represents this phase: the dependence of the colonized on the colonizer is noted, and a theory is evolved to explain it. The "colonizability" of the colonized is said to derive from the dependent relationships fostered by ancestor worship and its complementary family system. The colonizer's true task, if he can be enlightened, is not to perpetuate and bask in dependence, but to assist in the birth of a full personality in the colonized, launching his ego upon the troubled ocean of the inferiority complex. He must learn to endure the trauma of abandonment and stabilize his personality through desperate achievements. He must learn, as Western man has learned, to live out the myth of Tom Thumb.

In the third stage the initiative passes to the colonized, whose stirrings—Garveyism, negritude—have ushered in the second stage. The dependence theory of Mannoni and other notions of "colonizability" are angrily and summarily rejected. Colonization itself is revealed as the creator of its dependents, and a full psychological analysis of the colonial situation is undertaken. The reader for whom Fanon and Memmi write their descriptions is the

> colonized man, the man who now seeks to re-make himself by destroying the
> situation which created him as colonized, and, in an expression which they
> both use, to "re-enter history." (121–22)

In an effective piece of rhetorical inversion, Kirkwood here rewrites the three phases identified by Fanon in the development of the national culture of indigenous peoples—namely, assimilation into the colonial culture, then reaction and immersion in the indigenous culture, followed by revolutionary commitment—from the point of view of the colonizer, who finds himself, as settler, having witnessed and lived through all three phases, with the effect that he grows in self-awareness as he observes himself being posited as the object of an emergent discourse of the colonized. This self-objectification is, of course, also a self-critique, and Kirkwood goes on to discuss some of the worst features of the colonizer self: what he calls "the Nero complex" ("Nero, the usurper of the birthright of Britannicus"); the relationships of intimacy which develop with the colonized but which are abused or repressed in the colonizer; the reliance on a language of dependence, full of imperatives and hierarchical modes of address; the mediocrity of colonial culture as the consequence of its provincial relationship with the metropolis; and the process whereby the colonizer ego is constituted on the assumption of superiority (125–31). The critique must eventuate, says Kirkwood, in self-transcendence, but he adds that "a life-technique, as well as an art-technique, will be required" (131–32).

In the year of the conference Poetry '74, Ravan Press—publisher of the SPRO-CAS reports and closely linked to the Christian Institute—brought out Coetzee's *Dusklands*. It, too, develops a critique of colonial history; moreover, it does so by positioning the subject within the colonial narrative and pursuing it through degrees of painful recognition and self-consciousness. Both in his mode of access to the culture and in his themes, in other words, Coetzee is an intimate and effective participant in opening up the new discursive possibilities. Yet his point of contact with these other developments is oblique. It is oblique because of personal history, for it came about through his exposure to America; it is oblique also because it is filtered by linguistic studies.

How does Coetzee's linguistic perspective factor into the revisionist moment? This is the question to be posed in turning to *Dusklands*. In the cultural estrangement of Texas, and linking different threads of his personal history and current situation, Coetzee brought aspects of his graduate studies to bear on the question of colonialism. In a sketch of the period written fifteen years later for the *New York Times Book Review* ("How I Learned about America") he tells of writing a paper for the linguist Archibald Hill on the morphology of Nama, Malay, and Dutch, exploring their interconnections by sifting through documents of colonial discourse such as travelers' reports of the territory of South West Africa, accounts of punitive raids against the Nama and Herero, anthropological and linguistic descriptions, and missionary and other historical records. The foundations of the critical technique of parody, which is developed in *Dusklands*, seem to have been laid here. In another essay written in Texas, Coetzee examined the syntax of exotic languages and discovered for himself "that every one of the 700 tongues of Borneo was as coherent and complex and intractable to analysis as English." He then speaks of the curious effect of generative grammar on his emerging ambition to write:

> I read Noam Chomsky and Jerrold Katz and the new universal grammarians and reached the point of asking myself: If a latter-day ark were ever commissioned to take the best that mankind had to offer and make a fresh start on the farther planets, if it ever came down to that, might we not leave Shakespeare's plays and Beethoven's quartets behind to make room for the last aboriginal speaker of Dyirbal, even though that might be a fat old woman who scratched herself and smelled bad? It seemed an odd position for a student of English, the greatest imperial language of them all, to be falling into. It was a doubly odd position for someone with literary ambitions, albeit of the vaguest—ambitions to speak one day, somehow, in his own voice—to discover himself suspecting that languages spoke people or at the very least spoke through them. ("How I Learned about America" 9)

The Chomskyan notion of deep structure, therefore, seems to have initiated Coetzee's drift away from either realist or romantic conceptions of authorial creativity. Instead of being the independent producer of literary language, the writer sets discourses in motion, pursuing their inner logic, sometimes setting several discourses in parallel—as in *Dusklands*, where the interest lies in the critical distance set up between different discourses. Coetzee's cultural displacement seems to have precluded him from taking up unreservedly the political model that Chomsky also represented; however, he was influenced, no doubt, by Chomsky's *American Power and the New Mandarins*, which, in questioning the role of "objective" scholarship in the context of the Vietnam War, is close to the concerns represented by Eugene Dawn's "mythography." All told, generative grammar seems to have enabled Coetzee to disconnect the notion of discourse from the autonomous subject of liberalism, a move confirmed by later reading in Continental structuralism and poststructuralism.

Coetzee's precursors in bringing linguistic studies into the field of colonial relations go back to the period of high imperialism and the work of orientalists such as Silvestre de Sacy and Ernest Renan. In Said's account in *Orientalism*, the successes of the orientalist philology of the nineteenth century included "comparative grammar, the reclassification of languages into families, and the final rejection of the divine origins of language"; these achievements, in Renan especially, linked orientalism definitively with the ideals of progress and scientific knowledge (135). Although Renan's "philological laboratory" was a significant contribution to the extension and consolidation of European discursive authority, Coetzee, projecting himself now into colonialism's dying moments, follows the tracks left by this tradition and finds evidence of cultural relativism. Coetzee's early linguistic studies, therefore, put him in touch with the source of the historical process he inwardly knows, enabling him to find Europe's authority dispersed and undermined in the deep structures of the languages of the nonmetropolitan world.

"The labyrinth of my history"

Dusklands and *In the Heart of the Country*

"My name is Eugene Dawn. I cannot help that. Here goes." The opening sentences of *Dusklands* present a subject abandoning itself to the necessities of its history. Similarly, Coetzee's early fiction involves a struggle with colonialism as defining the oppressive but ineluctable conditions of existence and self-consciousness.

Dusklands comprises two parts. Part 1, "The Vietnam Project," is the narration of Eugene Dawn, mythographer for the American presence in Vietnam. Dawn is writing a report on propaganda methods whose ultimate readership is the Department of Defense. Part 2, "The Narrative of Jacobus Coetzee," is the story of an elephant hunter and adventurer in conflict with the indigenous Khoisan of the Western Cape in South Africa. The novel therefore juxtaposes subject-positions within twentieth-century American imperialism and eighteenth-century Dutch colonialism, finding them coextensive in their quest for self-realization through dominance. Parody is the principal method of critique in both parts.[1] In part 1 the parodied documents are the work of what Chomsky in the context of Vietnam called "the backroom boys," the military bureaucrats and planners in corporations allied to the Department of Defense. In part 2 the parodied documents are drawn from the archives of colonial expansion published by the Van Riebeeck Society in South Africa.

One of the first ruses of all colonial self-representations is to find ways of harmonizing and naturalizing the relationship of the colonist to the new landscape and its inhabitants (*White Writing* 8); seen in this light, Coetzee's candid return to colonialism's founding moments of violence represents an attempt to break through the crust of contemporary ideology. The two parts of *Dusklands* disturb, first, American self-confidence concerning the global defense of democracy (a policy consolidated during the Truman administration and given considerable effect under Kennedy: Eugene Dawn writes his Vietnam Report for the Kennedy Institute in the Harry S. Truman Library) and, second, the only slightly more fantastical white South African presumption about representing a historical link with Western, civilized values on a barbaric continent, a notion fed by the mythology of the frontier. A noteworthy feature of this critique is Coetzee's refusal to offer an easy vantage point from which one might gaze on the fictional subject in full self-possession: the narrating subject resides *in* its history. Because no other time frame is given in which readers might position themselves—as with Fredric Jameson's model of the political unconscious, history is known to us only in its effects, in the language in which the subject speaks—the critique strikes home, addressing itself to the naturalized structures that maintain their hold over the contemporary consciousness.[2]

Ideologically sensitive critics of *Dusklands* have registered misgivings about the juxtaposition of Dawn in the context of the Vietnam War and Jacobus Coetzee in the context of eighteenth-century Dutch colonialism at the Cape.[3] We should be cautious, however, about taking such misgivings to their obvious polemical conclusion, that is, to the point of inferring that Coetzee wishes to mount a philosophically idealist diagnosis of Western imperialism. In both narratives, solipsism and narcissism, the pitfalls of philosophical idealism, are seen explicitly in terms of the colonist's failure to engage in reciprocal relationships; moreover, Jacobus Coetzee's metaphysics of the gun ("guns save us from the fear that all life is within us" [84]) is more than metaphysical: it suggests an impoverished ethic.

The two narratives are connected, however, not only by their thematic resemblance but more substantially by the sense of displacement and complicity that Coetzee begins to feel as a white South African with an Afrikaner pedigree studying in Texas during the escalation of the Vietnam War. Coetzee has said that complicity was not in question at the time: "Complicity was far too complex a notion for the time being—the problem was with knowing what was being done. It was not obvious where one went to escape knowledge" ("How I Learned about America" 9). But complicity is what the novel, written four or five years later, undertakes to explore: Coetzee connects his ancestry and current experience, finding ways of making sense of the contiguity of American and Dutch imperialism in determining his *own* historical situation.[4] The connections are established, in other words, in the act of authorship itself.

THE CRITIQUE OF RATIONALITY

A specific social identity is interrogated in *Dusklands* by means of a parodic replication of historical documents. The spirit of rebellion in *Dusklands* has been seen by Michael Vaughan as a revolt against liberal positivism and a rejection of the aesthetics of liberal realism ("Literature and Politics" 126). Broadly, I agree with these observations; however, Coetzee also goes back to the sources of this positivism and conducts a double-edged critique: first, he historicizes it with reference to the history of philosophical rationalism; second, he exposes the subject-positions and ethical duplicity that are masked by rationalism's objectivist pretensions.

Historicization takes the form of returning positivism to the moment of Western scientific rationality, essentially to Descartes. Hugh Kenner's description of Beckett's parody of Cartesian rationality helps in defining this aspect of Coetzee's project more closely:

> The Beckett trilogy [*Molloy, Malone Dies*, and *The Unnamable*] takes stock of the Enlightenment, and reduces to essential terms the three centuries during which those ambitious processes of which Descartes is the symbol and progenitor (or was he too, like The Unnamable, spoken through by a Committee of the *Zeitgeist?*) accomplished the dehumanization of man. The Cartesian Centaur [the cyclist, representative of a perfect harmony of mind and body-as-machine] was a seventeenth century dream, the fatal dream of being, knowing, and moving like a god. In the twentieth century he and his machine are gone, and only a desperate élan remains: "I don't know, I'll never know, in the silence you don't know, you must go on, I can't go on, I'll go on." (132)

Unlike Beckett, however, Coetzee does not allow the skeptic's reconstruction of the *cogito* to lead to an empty space where form must register pure doubt and where all attempts to produce meaning appear clownish or vacuous; in Coetzee the process is taken in the direction of seeing the founding philosophical moments in world-historical terms. These terms include both the observation that the period of scientific ascendancy coincides with colonial expansionism and the conviction that in the twentieth century the process is coming to an end with decolonization; the beginning of the process is therefore seen from the perspective of its end. Hence, in the allegory of names in the first part of *Dusklands*, "Dawn," as the supposedly autonomous "I" of what is also the bourgeois moment, the moment of Crusoe, finds himself in the "dusklands" of history, attempting to reestablish a crumbling edifice by means of the "New Life Project."[5] "The Vietnam report," says Dawn, "has been composed facing east into the rising sun and in a mood of poignant regret (*poindre*, to pierce) that I am rooted in the evening lands" (7). In the second part of *Dusklands* the violence associated with the assertion of scientific rationality in the colonies is explored in various forms, both epistemic and physical. The eighteenth-century frontiersman Jacobus Coetzee (in the archival sources, a grandson of the original Coetzee burgher who arrived from Holland in 1679 and settled in what is now Stellenbosch) also registers the pressures of twentieth-century African nationalism and anticolonialism. Coetzee's whole framework therefore anticipates closely Jameson's more recent account of the beginnings of the 1960s—as a period of diverse and fundamental shifts or "breaks" of consciousness—in Third World movements toward decolonization ("Periodizing the 60s" 180–86).

The two philosophers mentioned most frequently as providing Coetzee with some of his terms in *Dusklands* are Hegel and Spengler. As Teresa Dovey and others have shown, the pertinent section of the *Phenomenology of Mind* is the master-slave dialectic. I shall turn to this dialectic more than once in this study, but it is necessary here to note that the master-slave dialectic ought to be seen in the light of Hegel's critique of essential Enlightenment concepts, a critique that shows that the consciousness of freedom—the highest goal of human thought—is impossible outside of social relations. Jameson shows the provenance of this theme in the 1960s in his discussion of Sartre's analysis of the Look in *Being and Nothingness*, an analysis that was later taken up by Frantz Fanon ("Periodizing the 60s" 188). Coetzee's Hegelianism in *Dusklands* participates in the same tradition; it is the means whereby the "ontological shock" produced by the presence of the Other under colonial conditions is registered.[6]

In the case of Spengler the connection has been thought to be largely titular, the idea of "dusklands" being derived from *The Decline of the West*. However, there might be more to Spengler's influence than this allusion. Spengler distinguishes *chronological* from *mathematical* number and "pragmatic" history from "the *morphological relationship* that inwardly binds together the expression-forms of *all* branches of a Culture" (6). Even in his use of linguistic analogy Spengler is a protostructuralist who would have been congenial to Coetzee's efforts to grasp systemic rules. But thematically Spengler is significant in his distinction between the *world as nature* and the *world as history*, which has behind it the classic Heideggerian distinction between being and becoming—to which Spengler connects nature/culture—and which leads to his description of the movement in Western history from culture to *civilization*. (In later novels Coetzee artfully uses such binary categories as structural mechanisms for the production of writing.) The movement in Western history from culture to civilization, from organic to inorganic relations, is marked in Spengler by the predominance of the world-city over the province and is fulfilled finally in imperialism: "Imperialism is Civilization unadulterated" (36). Appropriately for the present context, the figure who embodies imperialism as "the first man of a new age" is Cecil Rhodes; according to Spengler, "The expansive tendency is a doom, something daemonic and immense, which grips, forces into service, and uses up the late mankind of the world-city stage, willy-nilly, aware or unaware" (37). Dawn's vision of progress develops from similar philosophical foundations and is in the end equally obsessive, doom laden, and self-aware:

> When I was a boy making my quiet way through the years of grade school I kept a crystal garden in my room: lances and fronds, ochre and ultramarine, erected themselves frailly from the bottom of a preserve-jar, stalagmites obeying their dead crystal life-force. Crystal seeds will grow for me. The other kind do not sprout, even in California. (32)

> But has the master-myth of history not outdated the fiction of the symbiosis of earth and heaven? . . . In the Indo-China Theater we play out the drama of the end of the tellurian age and the marriage of the sky-god with his parthenogene daughter-queen. If the play has been poor, it is because we have stumbled about the stage asleep, not knowing the meaning of our acts. Now I bring their meaning to light in that blinding moment of ascending metahistorical consciousness in which we begin to shape our own myths. (28)

In addition to historicization, the other method employed in Coetzee's attack on rationality is the laying bare of the narrator's subject-position. The parodic effect here takes in the scientific discourses that have evolved in the wake of the Enlightenment; these discourses, in one way or another concerned with enlarging empirical knowledge, are the principal means whereby the narrators attempt, on behalf of their cultures, to manage their world and achieve self-affirmation and mastery. The tools evolving in post-Beckett metafiction were at hand in this aspect of Coetzee's work; the example of Vladimir Nabokov's *Pale Fire* is particularly relevant, with its specious scholarship and combination of text and commentary. In *Dusklands* the method is extended to a proliferation of texts and countertexts, which enables Coetzee to hold up various discourses for objectification.

"Mythography," in "The Vietnam Project," is the first of Coetzee's parodic targets; it is also the most difficult to account for because it is an analytical discourse still in the making at the time, with some resemblance to structural functionalism: "Mythography," says Dawn, " . . . is an open field like philosophy or criticism because it has not yet found a methodology to lose itself in the mazes of. When McGraw-Hill brings out the first textbook of mythography, I will move on" (33). The passage goes on to develop a direct analogy between mythography and colonial exploration, with the implication that what Dawn undertakes as a contemporary intellectual enterprise is a later and more abstract version of what Jacobus Coetzee undertakes in the interior of Southern Africa. As the analysis of myths and the ways in which cultures depend on them, mythography projects metacritical, metanalytical powers that can be mobilized in the service of domination.[7] In "The Narrative of Jacobus Coetzee" other discourses come into focus. Narratives of colonial exploration and adventure, descriptions of landscape and manners and customs, and frontier or pioneer history deepen and localize Coetzee's critique, revealing the legacy of key colonial discourses in the ideological management of Southern Africa. I now turn to Coetzee's sources; in both parts of the novel Coetzee alters the original documents in such a way as to shatter the composure of the subject's self-representation.

PARODY: THE AMERICAN CONTEXT

In "The Vietnam Project" the original documents appear to be taken from a series of studies on "national security and international order" put together by the Hudson Institute, which published a volume entitled *Can We Win in Vietnam? The American Dilemma* (Armbruster et al.). The book was completed in the aftermath of the Tet offensive in February 1968, when the Viet Cong inflicted severe damage on South Vietnamese and American installations, fueling domestic anxiety in the

United States about the feasibility of pursuing the war. Of the five contributors to this volume, three were in favor of stepping up operations, and two thought the United States should cut its losses and get out. The introduction by Herman Kahn, a member of the prowar group, provided Coetzee with his epigraph:

> Obviously it is difficult not to sympathise with those European and American audiences who, when shown films of fighter-bomber pilots visibly exhilarated by successful napalm bombing runs on Viet-Cong targets, react with horror and disgust. Yet, it is unreasonable to expect the U. S. Government to obtain pilots who are so appalled by the damage they may be doing that they cannot carry out their missions or become excessively depressed or guilt-ridden. (Armbruster et al. 10)

Unreasonable is the key word here, illustrating the spirit of cool, technological equanimity that Dawn aims for in his report—unsuccessfully, of course. By contrast, Kahn is successful, discussing at some length the "instrumental" position of tying the moral issues with the question of whether the war is actually winnable (204). The rhetorical situation in "The Vietnam Project" relies on the example of the Hudson documents (of course, other corporations, such as Rand, offered similar services). Dawn is a backroom boy who, like several of the Hudson strategists, offers a program for improving the effectiveness of the American war effort. In matters of substance, moreover, the debates being conducted in the Hudson Institute prepare the way for Coetzee. For example, there is much discussion in *Can We Win in Vietnam?* of cultural factors as being potentially decisive in determining the war's outcome. The more forthright of the critics of U.S. policy, Edmund Stillman, put the case as follows:

> Vietnam is a land of strange and violent sects—e.g., Cao Dai and Hoa Hao, "religions" that are also armed movements, and such "criminal sects" like the Binh Xuyen, Mafias with religious overtones. All unwittingly, America has stumbled into a strange and convulsed society—and one that makes a mockery of the traditional American world view, still faithful to its eighteenth-century Enlightenment origins and its nineteenth-century belief in the ability of material wealth to calm any disorder of the spirit. (Armbruster et al. 156)

Coetzee unravels this apprehension—revealing the Euro-American "disorder of the spirit" that Stillman claimed is under control—in Cartesian and Hegelian terms, thus giving it content and a philosophical and critical explanation. Rounding off the argument for withdrawal, Stillman quoted Santayana in vocabulary directly applicable to Dawn: "A fanatic is one who, having lost sight of his object, redoubles his zeal" (164). Kahn, in opposing critics such as Stillman, argued in favor of seeing the problem in Vietnam as a purely technical matter and as one of having a "theory of victory" (Armbruster et al. 204–12). As Dawn puts it in *Dusklands*: "There is only one problem in Vietnam and that is the problem of victory. The problem of victory is technical. We must believe this. Victory is a matter of sufficient force, and we dispose of sufficient force" (29).

On occasion, the advocates of military solutions at the Hudson Institute came close to the threshold of moral discretion. For example, Kahn argued that there "may be in this kind of war vital special operations that do not meet these [Geneva Convention] criteria. If so, I would recommend, first, that they be isolated from regular military operations, and secondly, that they be rigorously reviewed and controlled at some reasonably high level" (Armbruster et al. 319–20). Gastil, in a plan for a revised "defense system" for areas controlled by the Viet Cong, suggested that the locals be placed in categories ranging from those to be tried for specific crimes (involving "punishment up to execution") to "persons permitted to live normally and take part in politics." Then he added, "It might well be found just, and certainly expedient, to place present VC cadres in all categories, with most of the people in the last" (Armbruster et al. 416). The acknowledgment of expedience here amounts to an acceptance of the strategic value of terror. Dawn is disgraced at the Kennedy Institute because he breaks this precise threshold repeatedly and explicitly. On one occasion he repeats Gastil's implication exactly: "Szell reports that a camp authority which randomly and at random times selects subjects for punishment, while maintaining the *appearance* of selectivity, is consistently successful in breaking down group morale" (25). More generally, Dawn's advocacy of a program of assassination and of area bombing transgresses the boundary separating tacit from explicit: "There is an unsettling lack of realism about terrorism among the higher ranks of the military. Questions of conscience lie outside the purview of this study. We must work on the assumption that the military believe in their own explanations when they assign a solely military value to terror operations" (23). Or again: "Until we reveal to ourselves and revel in the true meaning of our acts we will go on suffering the double penalty of guilt and ineffectualness" (31).

An important part of Dawn's report, and the ultimate application of his mythography, is to argue for the broadcasting of radio propaganda that manipulates the psychic reflexes built into traditional Vietnamese culture. Such a strategy is merely the logical extension of the kind of observation offered by Kahn in a contribution entitled "Toward a Program for Victory":

> The problem is not to convert the average Vietnamese to our own image, but to work with the materials at hand. This, of course, may mean attempting to fulfill certain aspirations for modernism that many Vietnamese have, but at the same time adapting our programs and policies to the existential situation—particularly the fact that most of our supporters are "peoples of the past" and not a superpoliticized, modern totalitarian movement such as the NLF [National Liberation Front]. (Armbruster et al. 341)

Dawn's science is able to make specific proposals in this direction: by presenting itself as the father figure and trying to instill doubt by means of the "father-voice," America only reinforces the traditional myth of rebellion of the band of brothers; therefore, Dawn argues, the programming must assert previously unknown forms of authority, preferably ones based on raw technological dominance.

A question worth raising here relates to the fact that there was much debate in the United States in the 1960s—reflected in the Hudson papers—about whether the dominant ideology in Viet Cong insurgency was communist or nationalist. The cold war thinking of the State Department under Kennedy clearly regarded the insurgency as communist, hence the commitment of troops; many critics of foreign policy, however, regarded the NLF as nationalist. Not all of those favoring the nationalist argument advocated withdrawal, as Kahn's position illustrates; this is Dawn's point of view as well. It is curious, though, that in Dawn's construction of Vietnamese myth there is no reference to the Marxist Leninism of the NLF, whose formulaic rigidity is more than exemplified in Ho Chi Minh's *Selected Writings*. Coetzee himself would have been conscious of the language of the NLF and the debate taking place in the United States.

The solution to this puzzle is to be found in the fact that Dawn's report owes much more to the notion of the "primal horde" in Freud's *Totem and Taboo* than to any respectable ethnographic description of Viet Cong or South Vietnamese traditions (which, when not influenced by Marxist Leninism, were quite heterogeneous, involving a range from

Catholic to Chinese Buddhist). Coetzee's decision simply to *ignore* what ethnography might tell him is surely deliberate, for the parodic effect depends on Dawn's perspective coming from *within* imperialism and its traditions (this positioning of the critique will develop as a consistent pattern in later novels); moreover, the decision dramatizes the fact that Dawn's epistemic framework encourages a Manichaean emphasis on cultural difference and the assertion of power.

PARODY: THE SOUTH AFRICAN CONTEXT

In part 2 of *Dusklands* Coetzee shifts attention from cultural anthropology to historiography. Eugene Dawn's counterpart is the editor and historian S. J. Coetzee, and his mythography is matched by S. J. Coetzee's white nationalist, pioneer history.[8] Significantly, the dates given for the fictitious course of lectures by S. J. Coetzee at the University of Stellenbosch, from which the afterword is drawn, precisely mark the period of the rise of formal political power of Afrikaner nationalism under D. F. Malan, from the break with the Smuts-Hertzog Fusion government in 1934 to final electoral victory in 1948. J. M. Coetzee is therefore largely concerned with the discursive resources and the legacy of that achievement.

"The Narrative of Jacobus Coetzee" is a collection of four documents: (1) the narrative itself, a first-person account of Jacobus Coetzee's journey and return; (2) the record of a second journey (also given by Jacobus Coetzee in the first person) under the leadership of Captain Hendrik Hop, amounting to a punitive raid on Jacobus Coetzee's deserted servants; (3) an afterword by S. J. Coetzee; and (4) an appendix, consisting of the "original" deposition or *Relaas* of 1760 by Jacobus Coetzee. As editor of Jacobus Coetzee's narrative and its official historian, S. J. Coetzee's role in the reproduction of historical data places him at the center of part 2; however, J. M. Coetzee, as "translator," is S. J. Coetzee's antagonist, for it quickly emerges that J. M. Coetzee subversively reproduces the work of S. J. Coetzee, both by dropping intertextual ironies and by actively rewriting the historical documents themselves; he thus explicitly breaks the conventionally neutral stance of translator.

The epigraph to part 2, "What is important is the philosophy of history," comes from a point in Flaubert's parodic *Bouvard et Pécuchet* when, having discovered the relatively arbitrary status of dates, the protagonists question the relevance of facts in general; this insight provides the momentary certainty of "Ce qu'il y a d'important, c'est la philosophie de l'Histoire!" (190). Very soon, however, Flaubert's characters discard even this formula for other opinions. In *Dusklands* the formula emphasizes the fickleness of data and directs attention to the struggle *over* history. It is interesting that Coetzee should have returned to *Bouvard et Pécuchet*; his more modest subversion of the archives of the Van Riebeeck Society has, as one of its points of origin, Flaubert's subversion of the scientific documents of the Enlightenment, especially the encyclopedia.

The source of S. J. Coetzee's version of pioneer history could have been provided by one N. A. Coetzee, who in 1958 published in the journal *Historia* an essay entitled "Jacobus Coetzee: Die Boerepionier van Groot-Namakwaland."[9] Whereas S. J. Coetzee is defensive and less than ingenuous (in the hands of J. M. Coetzee), the actual N. A. Coetzee is forthright in his treatment of the ancestral frontiersman: "Jacobus Coetzee was een van die merkwardigste persoonlikhede in ons pioniersgeskiedenis" (one of the most noteworthy figures in our pioneer history; 588). N. A. Coetzee drops phrases such as *die binneland oop te maak* (to open the interior), *die voorposte van die beskawing* (the outposts of civilization), and *die wye onbekende van 'n eie vaderlandsbodem* (a profound oxymoron, literally, "the wide unknown of one's own native soil") (593). Most pertinently, N. A. Coetzee argues that Jacobus Coetzee was resourceful in finding ways of exercising his "gesag as blanke . . . in 'n see van barbare" (authority as a white man in a sea of barbarians) when he approached the "Great Namaquas." His strategy involved keeping out of their camp, claiming the authority of the governor, and negotiating for safe passage in the vernacular (595). This version of the encounter, in relation to the experience of other explorers in the region, notably Carel Fredrik Brink and Hendrik Jacob Wikar, is *atypically* confrontational, but it is nevertheless N. A. Coetzee's account that endures in the parodic version in *Dusklands* itself (69–73). J. M. Coetzee's use of sources, in other words, would seem to be directly related to his critical intentions with respect to white nationalism, which found the confrontational version useful to its purposes.

It has been assumed since Peter Knox-Shaw's discussion of Coetzee's sources that the deposition or *Relaas* of Jacobus Coetzee (reproduced as an appendix to the novel) is the one authentic historical document in *Dusklands* and that the remaining sections are either fictitious or deliberately corrupted (27). This assumption is inaccurate, however, for Coetzee tampers substantially with the deposition as well. Apart from

minor but consistent alterations in dates and figures, Coetzee significantly omits from and adds to the document. Omitted (among other
details that disturb narrative coherence) are references to the friendly
disposition of the Namaquas; the fact that Jacobus Coetzee was allowed
to pass through the territory without interference; that there was an
exchange of gifts (oxen for links from his trek-chain; Wikar 285); and,
finally, that he returned *with one of the Namaquas* who wished to get to
the Cape (289)! (Needless to say, N. A. Coetzee omits most of these
details as well, since they detract from the confrontational emphasis.)
Still more startlingly, *added* to the deposition (in suitably imitative
language) are two accounts of desertion, one involving an "envoy of the
Damroquas [who] had not long ago met a treacherous end at the hands
of servants afflicted for lack of pursuits with the Black Melancholy; that
these servants had fled to the Namaquas he the narrator had first met
and dwelt yet among them" (*Dusklands* 132). The other instance involves an episode in which Jacobus Coetzee was "deserted by his servants but not . . . disturbed by the aforementioned Namaquas" (133).

J. M. Coetzee therefore omits cordial exchanges from the record and
adds desertion. The immediate purpose would seem to be to engineer a
certain consistency: Jacobus Coetzee's first-person narrative at the start
of part 2 also includes an episode of desertion. The deeper and more
salient purpose, however, is that these alterations radically turn the
narrative into a game of power. Desertion and its consequences are key
components of the movement of the colonizer-self as it runs from
assertion to debilitation, with Jacobus Coetzee delivering punishment to
the wayward servants in an attempt to reconstitute his authority.

I shall track this movement more carefully in what follows, but the
game of power would explain another, equally spectacular alteration.
The actual Hop expedition was a fact-finding mission prompted by the
original Coetzee's *Relaas* to investigate the economic prospects in the
territory and to locate a people (the Herero) who "are tawny in appearance, with long hair on their heads and are clad in linen, and who it must
be supposed are a civilised People" (Brink and Rhenius 5). J. M. Coetzee
ignores this original purpose (although he uses details from the Brink
expedition in constructing Jacobus Coetzee's narrative), making it a
punitive raid on the servants who have taken up with the Namaquas. In
rewriting the facts of the Hop expedition in this way, Coetzee seems to
have picked up two specific incidents in the events of the actual journeys
and conflated them. The first is the murder, during the return journey of
the Hop expedition, of a servant named Ruyter by a certain Coenraad

Scheffer (in the novel, "Scheffer" rivals only Jacobus Coetzee in sadism). Ruyter refused an order to fetch water and a struggle developed in which he was stabbed; later the same night, Scheffer shot Ruyter while everyone was asleep. The official narrative of the expedition was amended to conceal the murder from the Chamber of Seventeen in Holland (Brink and Rhenius vii, 115). The second incident concerns an illegal trading expedition (twenty-two years before Jacobus Coetzee's) by a party of burghers; the fact of the expedition was discovered by the authorities when, on the return journey, the Hottentot servants, "with or without their masters' permission, returned armed, and robbed the Great Namaquas, killing seven of them" (Brink and Rhenius 94). As in "The Vietnam Project," in other words, J. M. Coetzee renders explicit what is relegated in the original documents to the borders of legality. "But I have nothing to be ashamed of," says Dawn; "I have merely told the truth" (38).

Knox-Shaw's objection that the "fictional narrative is distinguished throughout by a virtual effacement of economic motive" (28)—a position that has held currency (it is repeated by Teresa Dovey and Peter Kohler)—seems misplaced, therefore, in the light of what the revision of sources *does* achieve. But the observation is incorrect even on its own terms. The very opening paragraph of "The Narrative of Jacobus Coetzee" deals with the social consequences of the shift in white settlement from burgher to trekboer in the political economy of the eighteenth century, consequences that involved a developing competitiveness between the Boers and Khoisan over land and cattle. The narrative begins with the story of Adam Wijnand, the son of a servant who left home and established himself with "ten thousand head of cattle, as much land as he can patrol, a stableful of women" (61); this tale locates Jacobus Coetzee's bitterness immediately and precisely within this context. If, as Kohler argues (24–25), the background to the story of Adam Wijnand is the history of Adam Kok, then we must deduce that it was precisely to contextualize Jacobus Coetzee in this way that J. M. Coetzee was once again so deliberately cavalier with the historical record, for Coetzee would be omitting Kok's political career in order to emphasize the contest over resources. Jacobus Coetzee himself mentions the object of his journey—to find ivory—when negotiating with the Great Namaquas (75). In S. J. Coetzee's afterword we are also told of Jacobus Coetzee, on the banks of the Great River, dreaming "a father dream of rafts laden with produce sailing down to the sea and the waiting schooners" (128). One might go so far as to say that the novel's

depiction of the material context is subtle enough to be able to plot
Jacobus Coetzee's economic options in terms of attempts to revive
earlier practices in the colonial enterprise (a raid on natural resources
followed by trade) in the face of the threat of impoverishment that the
shift from mercantile capitalism to settler pastoralism entailed in the
political economy of the Western Cape in the eighteenth century. It
would be more accurate to say, however, that Coetzee's interests simply
lie elsewhere.

THE QUEST FOR POWER:
ASSERTION, PRESERVATION, RECOVERY

"The one gulf that divides us from the Hottentots is our Christianity,"
says Jacobus Coetzee. "We are Christians, a folk with a destiny. . . . The
Hottentot is locked into the present. He does not care where he comes
from or where he is going" (61–62). This categorical emphasis on
difference is reinforced in subsequent descriptions of commando raids
against the "Bushmen" (62–66).[10] The final paragraph in these descriptions deals with the rape of Bushmen women, which Jacobus Coetzee
represents as offering an ideal of freedom, "the freedom of the abandoned": unlike the colonists' daughters, who connect the white male
with "a system of property relationships," a "wild Bushman girl is tied
to nothing": "You have become Power itself now and she is nothing, a
rag you wipe yourself on and throw away" (65). Shortly I shall discuss
the aggression that surfaces in Coetzee's prose in *Dusklands*, as it does
in this instance; for the moment, let me simply refer to this as a fiction of
self-assertion on Jacobus Coetzee's part. That it is a *fiction* soon becomes apparent: immediately hereafter, the narrative proper begins
(under the heading "Journey Beyond the Great River"), with J. M.
Coetzee putting together from Brink's journal a cursory account of the
journey northward that he might get to the encounter with the Great
Namaquas as quickly as possible. In this encounter and what follows,
the fiction of self-assertion is destroyed—and has to be restored, in the
final episode, at all costs.

   In the initial moments of the encounter Jacobus Coetzee sizes up the
Namaqua leader and is condescendingly pleased with his self-assurance
and humanity (this is the Hegelian pleasure of extracting self-validation
from the recognition given by the Other), but J. M. Coetzee lingers here,
departing from the narrative used in the construction of the journey in

order to delve more fully into the resonance of the moment by means, once again, of an explicit parody:

> Tranquilly I traced in my heart the forking paths of the endless inner adventure: the order to follow, the inner debate (resist? submit?), underlings rolling their eyeballs, words of moderation, calm, swift march, the hidden defile, the encampment, the graybeard chieftain, the curious throng, words of greeting, firm tones, Peace! Tobacco! , . . . the order to follow, the inner debate, the casual spear in the vitals (Visconte d'Almeida), the fleeing underlings, pole through the fundament, ritual dismemberment in the savage encampment, . . . the order to follow, the inner debate, the cowardly blow, amnesia, the dark hut, bound hands, uneasy sleep, dawn, the sacrificial gathering, the wizard, the contest of magic, the celestial almanac, darkness at noon, victory, an amusing but tedious reign as tribal demi-god, return to civilization, with numerous entourage of cattle—these forking paths across that true wilderness without polity called the land of the Great Namaqua where everything, I was to find, was possible. (70–71)

Strands are woven together here from a range of sources in colonial discourse, from chronicle and ethnography (such as the references to the death of d'Almeida and to methods of impaling imputed to Shaka) to adventure fiction (as in the wizard and the contest of magic, reminiscent of Rider Haggard's *King Solomon's Mines*). Framing the whole passage is the Conradian emphasis on the psychic journey inward—"the inner adventure"—and on the disappearance of known social conventions, with the implication that these genres of colonial discourse serve to confirm the subject's coherence and authority (while the "forking paths" also mischievously suggest the equivocal nature of the enterprise).

In several ways the preamble to Eugene Dawn's report contains similar attempts at self-assertion, though in Dawn's case the equivocation is more obvious. The account of the relationship with Marilyn (like Marilyn Monroe, the name of conjugal bliss) is a catalogue of failures to achieve connection, sexual and otherwise. Likewise, the photographs of prisoners, which Dawn carries around in his briefcase and regularly fetishizes, involve attempts to get beyond the surface of the picture to actual presence: "Under the persistent pressure of my imagination . . . it may yet yield" (17). The glint in the eye of the prisoner in the photograph is immediately generalized to all the Viet Cong, while Dawn speaks on behalf of his culture: "We brought them our pitiable selves, trembling on the edge of inexistence, and asked only that they acknowledge us" (18). American violence, imaged in guns, fire, a knife, and finally rape, is then projected as a hysterical attempt at self-validation in relation to the Viet Cong (18). Just as the structure of Jacobus Coetzee's narrative undermines his self-assertive fiction, so Dawn's attempts to contain his insecurity in the studied objectivity of the report go awry: "I am in a bad way as I write these words. . . . But I see things and have a duty toward history that cannot wait" (31).

Jacobus Coetzee is undermined early in his encounter with the Namaquas. In direct contrast to N. A. Coetzee's representation of Jacobus Coetzee's rhetorical skills in the local language, we find Jacobus himself acknowledging ruefully, "The irony and moralism of forensic oratory, uneasily translated into Nama, were quite alien to the Hottentot sensibility" (75). Things come to a head when he returns to his wagon to find the servants helpless while the locals pilfer his goods. He lays about him with a whip and the people retreat, but then a woman comes forward to taunt him; he fires into the ground at her feet and scrambles away with his men and oxen. Later that night a fever sets in, however, and the servants return him to the camp to seek help, thus subjecting him to a mild form of captivity. In his delirium Jacobus Coetzee meditates on self-preservation, using the language of metaphysics; like Eugene Dawn, Jacobus Coetzee thus becomes Herakles roasting in the poisoned shirt of Western heroic individualism (34).

The meditations begin with Jacobus Coetzee trying to define himself in terms of an isolated potency: "A great peace descended upon me: the even rocking of the wagon, the calm sun on the tent. I carried my secret buried within me. . . . I deepened myself in a boyhood memory of a hawk ascending the sky in a funnel of hot air" (80). He hears two voices, "one near, one far. 'Wash my feet, bind my breast,' said the near voice, 'will you promise not to sing?' Far away, from the remote South, the second voice sang" (80). These voices correspond to what S. J. Coetzee later will call "zones of destiny" (116): the near voice represents the appeal of the interior, now modified as an impulse to relinquish assertion and seek reconciliation; the far voice, the voice of the South, represents settlement or civilization. Caught between these zones in an indeterminate cultural space, Jacobus Coetzee must find ways of achieving self-consciousness as an integral being. J. M. Coetzee grants him the language of metaphysical speculation, but it is always inconclusive and, indeed, laconically ironized in the rhetorical context, for the meditations are addressed to "Jan Klawer, Hottentot," with his "savage birthright" (87).

The first of these meditations turns on the explorer's relationship with the landscape. Projecting himself outward from his bed to "repossess my world," Jacobus Coetzee realizes that "under the explorer's hammerblow this innocent interior transforms itself in a flash into a replete, confident worldly image of that red or grey exterior." Not only do the lures of the interior appear as "fictions," but he also has misgivings about his own "interior" being equally insubstantial: "My gut would dazzle if I pierced myself. These thoughts disquieted me" (83). The second meditation, on dreams, is similarly disconcerting. Jacobus Coetzee attempts, without much conviction, to recover the *cogito* in "a universe of which I the Dreamer was sole inhabitant," but he ends by questioning this proposition as "a little fable I had always kept in reserve to solace myself with on lonely evenings, much as the traveller in the desert keeps back his last few drops of water, choosing to die rather than die without choice" (83). The third meditation is on the subject of boundaries, of how the explorer, in seemingly limitless space and solitude, separates himself from his world. The primary defense against solipsism is the gun: "The gun is our mediator with the world and therefore our saviour. The tidings of the gun: such-and-such is outside, have no fear. The gun saves us from the fear that all life is within us" (84). His argument here is clearly self-defeating, as Dovey has shown (*Novels of J. M. Coetzee* 92–93), because if Otherness is eliminated by violence there can be no recognition of the subject.

When, in the final meditation, Jacobus Coetzee speaks about the approach of the master and savage toward one another across space, J. M. Coetzee is using Hegel in terms close to the original (Dovey, *Novels of J. M. Coetzee* 94). However, a distinction is necessary: in Coetzee we do not have master and slave, but master and *savage*. The Other, prior to his appearance as slave, is the Manichaean Other, with cultural difference inscribed in his Otherness, so that his approach involves the establishment of a *threshold* near which the explorer feels a genuine vulnerability. It is this threshold that presents itself to the explorer as "an ideal form of the life of penetration" (86). If the savage crosses the "annulus" to enter the master's space, he becomes slave, the Hegelian "inessential consciousness." But it is more frequently the case that there is no crossing of this limit; instead, there is an obligatory exchange of gifts, directions, warnings, demonstrations of firearms, followed by an enigmatic pursuit of the explorer, producing "the obscure movement of the soul (weariness, relief, incuriosity, terror)" that is felt as "a fated pattern and a condition of life" (86–87). Suspension, irresolution, anxiety: such is the explorer's existential lot.

We have come a long way, therefore, from the crisply efficient prose of the historian S. J. Coetzee: a broken and historicized subjectivity has intruded and subverted the record even before S. J. Coetzee's version of events is presented. The same pattern is found in "The Vietnam Project," where Dawn breaks off the bureaucratic register, saying, "We are all somebody's sons. Do not think it does not pain me to make this report" (28). He later adds that he is speaking "to the broken halves of all our selves," telling them "to embrace, loving the worst in us equally with the best" (31).

With his meditative delirium over, Jacobus Coetzee steadily "recovers." The recovery is organized around two features of the narrative, the rebellion of the servants, notably Plaatje, and the milking of the carbuncle. (This is surely among the most portentous of carbuncles anywhere.) The rebellion leads to desertion, the final and decisive challenge to Coetzee's authority; the carbuncle is a blessing, for *self-inflicted pain* enables Jacobus Coetzee to reconstitute himself as an object of consciousness. The theme is taken up in a later narcissistic reverie:

> Around my forearms and neck were rings of demarcation between the rough red-brown skin of myself the invader of the wilderness and slayer of elephants and myself the Hottentot's patient victim. I hugged my white shoulder, I stroked my white buttocks, I longed for a mirror. Perhaps I would find a pool, a small limpid pool with a dark bed, in which I might stand and, framed by the recomposing clouds, see myself as others had seen me, making out at last too the lump my fingers had told me so much about, the scar of the violence I had done myself. (103)

During the return journey to the Cape, Jacobus Coetzee's primary concern is to achieve a state of absolute self-sufficiency; of course, such a condition is illusory, and Jacobus Coetzee is perhaps at his most specious in this sequence. After being banished for biting off the ear of a child who taunted him, he turns necessity into a virtue by treating the loss of his wagon, weapons, accoutrements, and servants as a "casting off [of] attachments" (99). The death of Klawer occurs at this point, an event that is repeated in different forms, illustrating the complete subordination of the "record" to Jacobus Coetzee's reassertion of self. Dovey points out how contradictory Jacobus Coetzee's efforts to achieve ontological independence are in this sequence: his attempt to perform the "ur-act" ends in impotence; his calling to God to witness his aloneness shows his dependence on an imagined consciousness for self-recognition; and his ditty, "Hottentot, Hottentot, / I am not a Hottentot," traps him precisely in the relational position from which he is trying to escape (Dovey, *Novels of J. M. Coetzee* 107–8).

Because Jacobus Coetzee's experience is so much in polarities, he invents a hypothesis to contradict it. This is the story of the Zeno beetle that has the gift of seeming infinitely resistant to attack. Zeno held that Being is undivided; the category "not is" is logically unknowable; abstract ideas of motion and plurality are impossible because distance can never be wholly erased; and whatever is plural can simply be numbered. Jacobus Coetzee comforts himself with Zenonian principles, thus forcing what has been a story of fragmentation into a private myth of wholeness and integrity.

On his arrival at the Cape, Jacobus Coetzee plays out an ironic reversal of colonial tropes. If the Hottentots had been "true savages," he might have had a more satisfying encounter with them, he decides. Defining "true savagery" as "a way of life based on disdain for the value of human life and sensual delight in the pain of others" (104), he exemplifies these attributes himself (Knox-Shaw 31). Entering the periphery of colonial property, he attacks a herd of cattle and wounds the herder; on arrival at his own farm, he falls on a lamb like "God in a whirlwind" and enters his house with the liver (106).

The Hop expedition, however, demonstrates Jacobus Coetzee's sadism with horrifying clarity. Its purpose is nothing less than to stage, in the form of a punitive raid, the drive toward self-consciousness on the part of the seemingly reconstituted, male, assertive self. The sequence is made up of violence theatrically ritualized in self-consciousness. Conventions of adventure writing are exposed for this purpose: "We descended on their camp at dawn, the hour recommended by the classic writers on warfare, haloed in red sky-streaks that portended a blustery afternoon" (107). We are also made to watch Jacobus Coetzee *observing himself perform* his acts of cruelty: "A muscle worked in my jaw," he says, comforting the dying Plaatje, whom he has just shot (113).

The corresponding attempt to regain self-conscious potency in "The Vietnam Project" is the motel sequence, in which Dawn abducts his son Martin and stabs him with a fruit knife as the police arrive. Writing self-consciously in the "present definite," Dawn muses over the possibility of finding a language in which the referent—himself—is not problematized but is instead projected into a stable world of immanent and verifiable things. He speaks appreciatively of names, especially of song-birds, plants, and insects, which seem to have fullness and self-sufficiency. "Like so many people of an intellectual cast, I am a specialist in relations rather than names. . . . Perhaps I should have been an entomologist" (37–38). Similar questions are raised about novelistic discourse: "I have *Herzog* and *Voss*, two reputable books, at my elbow, and I spend many analytic hours puzzling out the tricks which their authors perform to give their monologues . . . the air of the real world through the looking-glass" (38). The books are well chosen, for together they imply a bildungsroman of the colonies; Dawn needs their realism in order to authenticate himself, though the very archness of his calculations excludes him from their promise, and the attempted self-recovery is inevitably a failure. Dawn's "true ideal," he tells us, rather like Jacobus Coetzee's Zenonian myth, "is of an endless discourse of character, the self reading the self to the self in all infinity" (40).

Dawn wonders whether a life of action would have saved him from his condition of self-division, but he realizes immediately that "men of action" have in fact created the history that is destroying him:

> I call down death upon death upon the men of action. Since February of 1965 their war has been living its life at my expense. I know and I know and I know what it is that has eaten away my manhood from inside, devoured the food that should have nourished me. It is a thing, a child not mine, once a baby squat and yellow whelmed in the dead center of my body, sucking my blood, growing by my waste, now, 1973, a hideous mongol boy who stretches his limbs inside my hollow bones, gnaws my liver with his smiling teeth, voids his bilious filth into my systems, and will not go. I want an end to it! I want my deliverance! (40)

The body situates the self within history, in this case a history comprising desperate acts of self-affirmation, undertaken in the encounter with the Other of Southeast Asia. Thus, a metonymic chain develops involving the body, the child-parasite, and the historical Other; it is this chain that Dawn tries to halt and destroy in stabbing the son, for the chain destroys the coherence of the transcendent self.

The violence of the Hop expedition in Jacobus Coetzee's narrative is so startling as to become a burden for many readers. Knox-Shaw, for example, indicts J. M. Coetzee on humanist grounds for merely reenacting "true savagery" and thereby furthering its claims (33). In response, Dovey points out that Coetzee is refusing the option of a neutralizing discourse (*Novels of J. M. Coetzee* 115). There is no question that the episode is projected specifically *as violence*:

> "Stand up," I said, "I am not playing, I'll shoot you right here." I held the muzzle of my gun against his forehead. "Stand up!" His face was quite empty. As I pressed the trigger he jerked his head and the shot missed. Scheffer was smoking his pipe and smiling. I blushed immoderately. I put my foot on Adonis's chest to hold him and reloaded. "Please, master, please," he said, "my arm is sore." I pushed the muzzle against his lips. "Take it," I said. He would not take it. I stamped. His lips seeped blood, his jaw relaxed. I pushed the muzzle in till he began to gag. I held his head steady between my ankles. Behind me his sphincter gave way and a rich stench filled the air. "Watch your manners, hotnot," I said. I regretted this vulgarity. The shot sounded as minor as a shot fired into the sand. Whatever happened in the pap inside his head left his eyes crossed. Scheffer inspected and laughed. I wished Scheffer away. (111)

Such writing is surely transgressive, not in a theoretical manner that enables one to explain it away, but in an *aggressive* mode that is aimed at readers' sensibilities. The formal explanation for these acts—what Jacobus Coetzee impatiently calls "expiation explanation palinode"—is given directly, and it is predictable: "Through their deaths I, who after they had expelled me had wandered the desert like a pallid symbol, again asserted my reality. . . . I have taken it upon myself to be the one to pull the trigger, performing this sacrifice for myself and my country-men, who exist, and committing upon the dark folk the murders we have all wished. . . . I am a tool in the hands of history" (113–14). A further reason, given by Jacobus Coetzee in explanation of his bitter-ness, is the "desolate infinity" of his power: undergoing "a failure of imagination before the void," he feels "sick at heart" (108–9). None of these explanations, however, is sufficient to account for the aggressive-ness of the prose. I would argue that the violence of the passage and others like it cannot satisfactorily be contained in interpretation, for the aggressiveness remains a *social* fact that readers have and will continue to give witness to. This argument relies on the description at the start of this chapter, in which Coetzee was said to be taking on, in a combative sense, the legacy of colonialism and its discourses; *Dusklands*'s explo-sive aggressiveness is a measure of the extent to which this struggle is not only with the conventions of fiction but also with the social and moral framework in which those conventions reside. The game of power is both a form of critical, historical diagnosis, and a fierce attack on the sensibility of literary humanism in South Africa.

THE EMERGENCE OF THE DISPLACED SUBJECT

Although aggressiveness is one of the consequences of Coetzee's fictive struggle with colonialism, another is the emergence of a displaced subject, a narrator who is not one of the primary agents of colonization but who lives in the conditions created by such agents, and who endures the subjectivity this position entails. Magda in *In the Heart of the Country* is such a displaced subject, but it is possible to discern its emergence in *Dusklands*. One of the explanations Jacobus Coetzee gives for his acts is that he is "a tool in the hands of history." After making this assertion, however, he has misgivings: "Will I suffer?" "I too am frightened of death." He dismisses these apprehensions as "a winter story" he uses to frighten himself and make the blankets more cozy, but then he closes with the following reflection:

> On the other hand, if the worst comes you will find that I am not irrevocably attached to life. I know my lessons. I too can retreat before a beckoning finger through the infinite corridors of my self. I too can attain and inhabit a point of view from which, like Plaatje, like Adonis, like Tamboer & Tamboer, like the Namaqua, I can be seen to be superfluous. At present I do not care to inhabit such a point of view; but when the day comes you will find that whether I am alive or dead, whether I ever lived or never was born, has never been of real concern to me. I have other things to think about. (114)

This conclusion straddles two possible positions: one poses the larger, existential questions, and another replies. The first position represents that aspect of J. M. Coetzee's authorial narration that would keep alive the options, either for escape—retreating down the corridors of the self—or for the shadings of moral receptivity and complexity. It is the position of the displaced subject. The second position, however, containing the reply, is one in which Jacobus Coetzee tries to shut off those options: "At present I do not care to inhabit such a point of view." It is possible, the paragraph suggests, that under different conditions Jacobus Coetzee might tell a different story of himself, a more subtle story, a story other than the ontological one of assertion, self-preservation, and recovery that we have been given, but only "when the day comes."

In its ambivalence this passage enacts a recognition followed by a denial of complexity. This movement is interesting in the work of a writer who values complexity almost to a fault. In this instance, however, Coetzee is developing a narrative subject who carries his own burdened fascination with, and antagonism toward, a part of his inherited culture. Complexity is curtailed by means of a gesture whose essential function is to preserve the moral imperative of the author's self-distancing from complicity and the imprisonment of naturalized connections. Jacobus Coetzee's gesture of denial or closure, in other words, amounts to a declaration of conscience on the part of J. M. Coetzee, one that says: this is the record; let us allow it to stand and speak for itself. It is for this reason, I believe, that J. M. Coetzee never again allows his authorship to inhabit a narrator as oppressive, as fatherlike, as Jacobus Coetzee. Later such figures are the *antagonists* of the narrators: Magda's father in *In the Heart of the Country,* or Colonel Joll in *Waiting for the Barbarians.* Such a narrator has to be inhabited for moral reasons, and appropriately at the start of the corpus, but in the end J. M. Coetzee must leave the Jacobus Coetzees to their own devices.

This is the meaning, I suggest, of the games of self-preservation played by Jacobus Coetzee on his return journey: "I had been set a task, to find my way home, no mean task, yet one which I, always looking on the brighter side of things, preferred to regard as a game or a contest" (104). The game of self-preservation is also J. M. Coetzee's game of surviving the narrative, pursuing its destructive logic to the end. After all, Jacobus Coetzee's games constitute a *mise en abîme,* a recounting of some of the sequences of the narrative itself: the journey, the punitive raid, captivity and expulsion, and a final game, "the most interesting one," a "Zenonian" approach toward death. "Would I be able to translate myself soberly across the told tale, getting back to a dull, farmer's life in the shortest possible time . . . ?" (105). Games of self-preservation are a small but important part of what fascinated Coetzee about Beckett; we know this from his commentary on *Watt,* but one might also recall Molloy's elaborate computations of how to rotate sixteen "sucking stones" from his mouth to the pockets of his trousers and greatcoat (*Molloy* 69–74). "In each game," says Jacobus Coetzee, "the challenge was to undergo the history, and the victory was mine if I survived it" (105). Similarly, victory for J. M. Coetzee is overcoming *Dusklands.*

In therapy, Dawn allows the analysts to trace their way through what he calls "the labyrinth of my history." The phrase neatly captures the authorial ambivalence I have been discussing. On the one hand, history is a maze of entrapments for the subject forced to inhabit it; on the other, it leads the doctors astray, providing protection for the subject's vulnerabilities. "My secret is what makes me desirable to you, my secret is what makes me strong. . . . Sealed in my chest of treasures, lapped in dark blood, it tramps its blind round and will not die" (49–50). Dawn's resistance to the therapists' attempts to explain him is representative of larger things in the Coetzee oeuvre; by the time he comes to write *Michael K*, Coetzee will have turned Dawn's "secret" into an affirmation of what is uncontainable in narrative discourse. In other words, if *Dusklands* is mainly diagnostic and critical in emphasis, it also finds a minor corner in which to position a different, displaced narrative subject, one that will develop and steadily find its own voice, or voices, in the corpus as a whole.

FICTIONALITY VERSUS THE HISTORICITY OF SELF

Magda in *In the Heart of the Country* is a "spinster with a locked diary" fighting against becoming "one of the forgotten ones of history" (3). The drama of this novel lies in Magda's attempts to find and speak a life for herself under such conditions, a life in which usual forms of exchange or relationship—from ordinary family bonding and sociability to marriage into colonial structures of kinship—seem either unauthentic or simply unavailable. Without the cultural mechanisms whereby a stable identity can be formed through the reflections of self thrown back by others, Magda speaks an obsessive interior monologue that rarely resembles a language of social intercourse.[11] The numbered units of her discourse reflect this lack of reciprocity; at the same time, they create the cinematic intensity associated with the *nouveau roman*, especially Robbe-Grillet's *Jealousy*.

Judging from Coetzee's translation and commentary on Gerrit Achterberg's sonnet sequence "Ballade van de gasfitter," he was bringing a diverse range of literary and philosophical sources to bear on the question of the self's relation to language and to others. These sources include Wallace Stevens ("Notes Toward a Supreme Fiction"), Martin Buber (*I and Thou*), Sartre (*Being and Nothingness*), and a tradition of reflexive fiction going back as far as Sterne. The immediate points of departure in Coetzee's essay, however, are linguistic descriptions in Emile Benveniste and Roman Jakobson of the unstable patterns of reference in pronouns and "shifters." Coetzee draws attention to the way these patterns govern the ontological and metaphysical significance that the terms *I* and *You* are made to carry. The similarities between the essay and the novel are striking, therefore: both take up questions of reciprocity and identity and their dependence on language, and both reflect on what Coetzee calls "the poetics of failure," a history of self-cancelling literature culminating in the "decline of the liberal-romantic notion of the self" ("Achterberg's 'Ballade van de gasfitter'" 293).

In important ways, however, the essay and the novel also part company. The essay describes a paradoxical effect of the "poetics of failure," in which the critique of notions of the self's autonomy retreats into a post-Romantic attempt to erect *the work itself* into ontological self-sufficiency. Where "nothing" is represented, the act of representing nothing is substituted; hence, Coetzee can say, "the poetics of failure is ambivalent through and through, and part of its ambivalence is that it must parade its ambivalence" (293). The novel participates in the poetics of failure to an extent, and in so doing it provides a parodic counterpoint to the traditions of liberal realism and pastoral in white South African fiction since Olive Schreiner (Dovey, *Novels of J. M. Coetzee* 149–68). Despite the transparency of conventions in the novel, there is no literary-ontological recuperation of the kind observed in the Achterberg poem. The closing sentences of the novel provide a convenient illustration of this difference: having wondered what other kinds of literature she might have constructed for herself, and having rejected the idea of inhabiting disingenuous forms of colonial pastoral, Magda says, "I have uttered my life in my own voice throughout, what a consolation that is, I have chosen at every moment my own destiny, which is to die here in the petrified garden" (138). As in Beckett, the appeal of an existential-historical realm of possibility, in which a palpable selfhood is hinted at, remains strong, even though the subject is never entirely free of the fear of arbitrariness or the depredations of irony. The field of *affect*, in other words, is never entirely eclipsed or neutralized by the field of language.

Coetzee's methods at this stage have something quite specific in common with the *nouveau roman*, namely, that the antirealist aesthetics of the movement were developed precisely in order to achieve a more "experiential" narration; for this reason the movement was also known as the *nouveau réalisme*. As Ann Jefferson puts it, the "natural air of narrative is false because it does not give us the world as it is, or as we experience it, and so must be condemned for its lack of realism" (15). Coetzee's novel is in fact close in spirit to the Robbe-Grillet described by

Jameson, who argues that a socially critical Robbe-Grillet appears in *Jealousy* through an existentialist treatment of colonial relations ("Modernism and Its Repressed" 173).

TRANSGRESSION AND THE EXPOSURE OF BOUNDARIES

Strictly speaking, very little "happens" in *Heart of the Country*. Despite several episodes of parricide and burial, at the end of the novel Magda is still serving her father weak tea and changing his napkins. For the most part, what happens is an act of consciousness and an act of language; what historicizes this act, however, is that it is deeply transgressive. I have discussed transgression of another kind in the violence of *Dusklands*'s prose; here, transgression has a larger function that I shall explore with reference to insights drawn from anthropology. As Mary Douglas shows in *Purity and Danger*, taboos define the boundaries of legitimate social behavior; when they are broken, these boundaries are revealed, together with the social structures they are designed to hold in place. Magda's is a transgressive consciousness that reveals the structures of relationship and authority—with their accompanying pathologies—of the settler-colonial context. "Acting on myself I change the world," she says. "Where does this power end? Perhaps that is what I am trying to find out" (36).

Magda's transgressions make up the sequential episodes in the narrative structure, with one sequence leading logically to the next in a pattern of conceptual reversals. Through Magda the novel forces the social codes to light, exposing them to scrutiny in the public domain of reading. The first sequence (sections 1–37) involves the family, and the distinguishing feature of the family structure in the novel is the absence of the mother. As with so much else, we cannot establish the "truth" about this absence: Magda speculates about her mother's death in childbirth following the father's relentless sexual demands (2). What is significant is that the absence of the mother throws Magda and her father into a relationship which—from Magda's point of view—has Oedipal implications. "Wooed when we were little by our masterful fathers, we are bitter vestals, spoiled for life. The childhood rape: someone should study the kernel of truth in this fancy" (3).

Two sets of consequences arising from the family situation may be discussed in anthropological terms. The first is the strengthening of the father's role as the bearer of what Bronislaw Malinowski calls the "principle of legitimacy" (59). "Legitimacy" here implies an identity and a name and provides a notion of order; thus, the father's role, in the absence of the mother, is to carry the historical destiny of the colonizer more deeply into Magda's consciousness of herself:

> And mother, soft scented loving mother who drugged me with milk and slumber in the featherbed and then, to the sound of bells in the night, vanished, leaving me alone among rough hands and hard bodies—where are you? My lost world is a world of men, of cold nights, woodfire, gleaming eyes, and a long tale of dead heroes in a language I have not unlearned. (7)

This reflection is prompted by Magda's recalling how much of her childhood was spent in the company of servants, where "at the feet of an old man I have drunk in a myth of a past when beast and man and master lived a common life as innocent as the stars and the sky" (7). In contrast to this folkloric idyll, colonialism involves severance from the mother of a relatively homogeneous culture and a descent into an alien and divided world of pioneers. The family structure is therefore also an allegory of the situation mentioned in the introduction to *White Writing*, in which white South Africans, having thrown off political, cultural, and finally moral ties with Europe, "from being the dubious children of a far-off motherland, . . . graduated to uneasy possession of their own, less and less transigent internal colony" (11).

The second consequence of Magda's family situation is what has been called "libidinal withdrawal" (Slater 111). Libidinal withdrawal is usually censured because it undermines the establishment of exogamous relations. Magda calls herself one of the "melancholy spinsters" who are "lost to history" because she has no role to play in reproducing the history, through marriage, which her father represents. Being lost to history means that she does not have access to a subject-position that is *inside* the history-making self-representations offered by the father.[12] His very possession of her, her entrapment, prevents such access; hence, "To my father I have been an absence all my life. Therefore instead of being the womanly warmth at the heart of this house I have been a zero, null, a vacuum towards which all collapses inward" (2).

When Magda opens the novel with the sentence "Today my father brought home his new bride," she does so from this vexed position. She is imagining the arrival of the bridal carriage because her father has been out courting, and she fears the worst—total displacement. Again, this is Magda's construction, but the truth it reveals is her sense of the position that history has allotted to her. Every minor development in the account of the arrival of the new wife is governed by this perspective: the wife of Magda's fantasy cuts her loose from the only intimate relationship she has and the only social identity she knows—both provided by the father—so the house becomes a "house with rival mistresses" (7). The ontological questions Magda poses for herself are generated *from within* these fears; they provide a culturally localized, affective framework in which the existential issues are situated: "What are pain, jealousy, loneliness doing in the African night? Does a woman looking through a window into the dark mean anything? I stare out through a sheet of glass into a darkness that is complete, that lives in itself. . . . There is no act I know of that will liberate me into the world. There is no act I know of that will bring the world into me" (9–10).

The first act of parricide, which occurs in the middle of the sequence, is presented as an attempt to break out of this impasse. It comes when Magda sees herself as the bearer of her father's child, with the child becoming an "Antichrist of the desert" leading a Hottentot rebellion against a settler town. In the daydream the rebels are "shot to pieces" and she concludes: "Labouring under my father's weight I struggle to give life to a world but seem to engender only death" (10–11). The imaginary killing of the bridal couple in their bed is a desperate rebellion against this death kiss of the father, against the rule of what he and his history represent to her.

The second sequence (sections 38–162) brings out the pathological *underside* of the colonial family, the relationships of intimacy and exclusivity between masters and servants. A principle of equivalence is set up between the family of the farmhouse and that of Hendrik when he brings home his new bride, Klein-Anna (as Magda calls her), in a passage that mirrors the opening of the novel: "Six months ago Hendrik brought home his new bride. They came clip-clop across the flats in the donkey-cart, dusty after the long haul from Armoede" (17). This structure of equivalence creates tensions that can be described in terms of two scenarios, both of which form the substance of later narrative developments: first, Magda's father will be substituted for Hendrik in the servants' marriage, and second, partly as a reprisal, Hendrik will be substituted for the father in the quasi-incestuous relationship with Magda.

The first scenario, which is the substance of the sequence, breaks the bar against miscegenation, unlocking liminal apprehensions in Magda as she confronts her father's illicit desires. The act of parricide in this sequence is the result of the father's *breaking* the rules rather than his *representing* them, as in the first instance; in other words, Magda rebels against both his duplicity and the duplicity of the conventions into which she has been socialized. Her imagination shows that exogamy as defined by the father involves parallel social structures that are supposed never to meet but that create the possibility, and indeed heighten the appeal, of easy sexual gratifications for men that are not ruled by institutionalized forms of exchange. (It is no wonder that Magda cannot take seriously the rituals of eyebrow plucking, tooth pulling, and fruit eating, though she contemplates them while staring in the mirror.) When Magda discovers this other world of illicit sexuality, she tries, in subsequent developments, to domesticate it by bringing Hendrik and Klein-Anna to live in the house and by entering willingly into a liaison with Hendrik. The attempt is hopeless and she is raped—the divisions proving more consequential than she had at first imagined.

After recounting the arrival of Klein-Anna, Magda's discourse turns on various aspects of epistemology and colonial history that are worth noting for their emphasis on social relations. Hendrik comes from the nearby township of Armoede (literally, "Poverty"), which Magda has never seen but is able to invent (though with some foreboding of a general retribution); having described the familiar social geography of poverty, Magda then says that what keeps her going is her determination to get beyond the "names, names, names" that separate her from this world, "to burst through the screen of names into the goatseye view of Armoede and the stone desert" (17). Later she recounts a "speculative history" in which she imagines the dispossession of Hendrik's forebears and the arrival of the first merino sheep to provide the economic base for settlement. She goes on to construct a dialogue in which Hendrik appeals for work at the farm: "'Wat se soort werk soek jy?' 'Nee, werk, my baas'" ("'What kind of work do you want?' 'No, just work, boss'"; 20). The use of Afrikaans is significant, because it implies a socially specific referencing whose most prominent features are later described by Magda after a similar dialogue with Klein-Anna: "A language of nuances, of supple word-order and delicate particles, opaque to the outsider, dense, to its children, with moments of solidarity, moments of distance" (30).

Magda's reflections, in the same sequence, on the relationship between desire and language also place social relations at the center: "Words are coin. Words alienate. Language is no medium for desire. Desire is rapture, not exchange. It is only by alienating desire that language masters it. . . . The frenzy of desire in the medium of words yields the mania of the catalogue" (26). Language is a social medium and a medium of exchange; desire is not—it is possession. This recognition underlies Magda's subsequent claim that she can represent sexuality: "How do I, a lonely spinster, come to know such things? It is not for nothing that I spend evenings humped over the dictionary." Words, the claim goes, can substitute for desire or serve as a defense against it. Her father has no such defense, but as a "dealer in signs," she has: "I pick up and sniff and describe and drop, moving from one item to the next, numbering the universe steadily with my words; but what weapons has he with which to keep at bay the dragons of desire?" (27). Similarly, because the language the father and Klein-Anna use in their lovemaking is public—"There is no private language. Their *jy* is my *jy* too" (35)— Magda feels that the rules of discourse on the farm will never be the same: "Whatever they may say to each other, even in the closest dead of night, they say in common words, unless they gibber like apes. How can I speak to Hendrik as before when they corrupt my speech?" (35).

Poised in this imaginative space, where, anticipating miscegenation, she is allowing the boundaries of knowledge and custom to be perforated on all sides, Magda undertakes some of her most intense ontological speculation. She makes recurring efforts to imagine herself as existing outside of human society, in what she calls her former state of "unthinking animal integrity" (40): she thinks of herself variously as "a thin black beetle with dummy wings who lays no eggs and blinks in the sun" (18); a snake "licking the eggslime off herself before taking her bearings and crawling off to this farmhouse to take up residence behind the wainscot" (38); or a black widow spider that would hide in a corner and "engulf whoever passes in my venom" (39). Still more poignantly, she sees herself inhabiting a world outside of consciousness altogether, the Sartrean being-in-itself: "This is what I was meant to be: a poetess of interiority, an explorer of the inwardness of stones, the emotions of ants, the consciousness of the thinking parts of the brain. It seems to be the only career, if we except death, for which life in the desert has fitted me" (35).

A related area of concentration in the sequence is her sense of an internalized absence of meaning. Although she has been "used as a tool" to run a farmhouse, she has another sense of herself "as a sheath, as a matrix, as protectrix of a vacant inner space" (41). Unlike her father, who appears like "a knifeblade cutting the wind, or a tower with eyes," she is "a hole with a body draped around it": "I am a hole crying to be whole" (41). The terminology is here is again specifically Sartrean; in the Achterberg essay Coetzee cites the description of consciousness in *Being and Nothingness* as "a hole through which nothingness pours into the world" (287). He also quotes Wallace Stevens's Nanzia Nunzio in terms that approximate Magda's condition: "I am the woman stripped more nakedly / Than nakedness . . . / Speak to me that, which spoken, will array me" (286).

Lacking such reciprocity, however, Magda's sense of self has to be created by autosuggestion, and her constructions bear out Coetzee's observations that "All versions of the *I* are fictions of the *I*. The primal *I* is not recoverable. . . . Indeed, after the experience of the Word in relation to one's existence, life cannot go on as before" (288). Producing fictions of the self from the image of a "hole," Magda concocts a "bucolic comedy" in which she features as wife to a farmer and mother to "a litter of ratlike, runty girls, all the spit image of myself, scowling into the sun, tripping over their own feet, identically dressed in bottlegreen smocks and snubnosed black shoes" (42). Alternatively, she imagines herself a high-minded defender of the feudal codes her father is busy destroying (43). Neither of these fictions is sustained very long, however, for she also sees herself hiding away in such constructions, in a passage that recalls the protective aspect of the labyrinth in *Dusklands*:

> It is the hermit crab, I remember from a book, that as it grows migrates from one empty shell to another. The grim moralist with the fiery sword is only a stopping place, a little less temporary than the wild woman of the veld who talks to her friends the insects and walks in the midday sun, but temporary all the same. Whose shell I presently skulk in does not matter, it is the shell of a dead creature. What matters is that my anxious softbodied self should have a refuge from the predators of the deep. (43–44)

A related attempt at self-preservation lies in Magda's efforts to create a story with "a beginning, a middle, and an end" (43). Her stories, which use the abandoned schoolhouse as a point of departure and involve a childhood with brothers and sisters learning together the rudiments of culture from a schoolmistress, are laced with arbitrariness.[13] The siblings quickly turn into horrible stepbrothers and stepsisters who ostracize her; one of them, "Arthur," is remembered as most beloved, although Magda explains that in fact he, too, showed her nothing but indifference. Magda's story gradually descends into collective culture, becoming steadily depersonalized in its association with fairy tales, such as the story of the Ugly Duckling, and the Arthurian legends. Later Magda will also reject psychological explanations of her condition, another form of storytelling, noting finally that all depends on the "old cold black wind that blows from nowhere to nowhere out of me endlessly" (64).

THE RECOVERY OF TEMPORALITY

Following the second parricide, in which Magda shoots her father clumsily through the window of the bedroom where he is making love to Klein-Anna, there are significant changes of narrative construction. Beginning in the second and developing in the third and fourth sequences, these changes involve, first, a dramatization of what Magda calls a changed "field of moral tensions," in which she has to rely on the servants' complicity in the murder, thus drawing them into an uncommon intimacy of shared knowledge and secrecy; this intimacy is taken further in Magda's decision to bring them into the house. Second, Magda senses that she is losing her grasp of time. The disorientation begins when she says: "A day must have intervened here. Where there is a blank there must have been a day during which my father sickened irrecoverably, and during which Hendrik and Klein-Anna made their peace" (79). The disorientation will eventually involve the recovery of a more conventional sense of time as the novel moves toward closure.

Indeed, Coetzee increasingly allows the passage of time to pressurize Magda. She begins to live "more and more intermittently," with blocks of time going missing. "Once I lived in time as a fish in water, breathing it, drinking it, sustained by it. Now I kill time and time kills me" (80). In the third sequence (sections 163–229) days are marked by sunsets and mornings, and the calendar makes an appearance for the first time, in the use of days of the week. There are also shifts of tense from present to past and back as Magda tries to regain her sense of the continuity of incident (114–15). Thus, Magda begins to lose her exclusive hold on the time of her fictive constructions—on the narrative perspective, that is, and the way time is controlled within it. At the simplest level this loss of control is apparent in her rising panic over the burial of her father after visitors have come to the farm; in a similar vein, Hendrik demands payment, and a boy arrives with a message demanding payment of taxes. Whereas in the opening sequence Magda's perspective on her father's desires determined the way time was represented, now Hendrik and the boy serve as additional agents of temporality.

Magda's loss of control over the narrative perspective and the self-affirming actions of Hendrik are, of course, thematically related. Coetzee is careful to repeat the rape sequence several times, thus denying it the status of an "event" and establishing it as a colonial fantasy on Magda's part, but it does suggest that Magda's is not the only history to be taken into account. The ghostly, ultimate referents of this act would seem to be decolonization and nationalism, registered obliquely through Magda's fears. Her efforts to get close to Klein-Anna, the rape itself, and subsequent fumblings over sexual partnership with Hendrik all ultimately fail, painful though they are: "There has been no transfiguration," she says. "What I long for, whatever it is, does not come" (113). Writing in the wake of the Soweto Revolt, Coetzee chooses to stress Magda's *failure* to transcend her alienation. Speaking of both Jacobus Coetzee and Magda, Coetzee said in an interview in 1978 that they "lack the stature to transform [the] 'It' into a 'You,' to, so to speak, create a society in which reciprocity exists; and therefore condemn themselves to desperate gestures towards establishing intimacy" ("Speaking" 23).

This sense of failure in *Heart of the Country* leads logically to the fourth and final sequence (sections 230–66), in which Magda displaces her efforts to achieve reciprocity to the realm of myth. The first sign that she intends giving up on the very possibility of human exchange, after Hendrik and Klein-Anna have abandoned the farm, comes when Magda frightens off the boy with the message about taxes. The child brings to mind the boy who appears at the end of each act of *Waiting for Godot*, claiming to have a message from Godot himself. The connection would imply that Magda is helpless before the demands of history and imprisoned in her own desires. Her need for community remains constant, however, to the extent that she speaks of a castaway who loses his mind because there is no one to talk back to him: "It is not speech that makes man man but the speech of others" (125). Her communion with the sky-gods is a substitute for this human communication and an attempt to find a language not mediated by social division.

The logic of the final sequence, perhaps even some of its stylistic ebullience, resembles Coetzee's description in the Achterberg essay of Buber's treatment of *I* and *You*:

> The existential incompleteness of the *I* is at the root of Martin Buber's myth of a primal *I-Thou* relation. The "primary word," says Buber, is not *I* but "*I-Thou*," the word of "natural combination" denoting a relation between *I* and *You* antedating the objectification of *You* into *It* and the isolation of *I* into being "at times more ghostly than the dead and the moon." This primal relation is, however, lost: "This is the exalted melancholy of our fate, that every *Thou* in our world must become an *It*." Intimations of the lost relation,

"moments of the *Thou* . . . strange lyric and dramatic episodes, seductive and magical, . . . tearing us away to dangerous extremes, . . . shattering security," inspire our efforts to reconstitute again and again the "between" of the primal *I-Thou*. (286)

Magda's efforts to communicate with the sky-gods involve an attempt to recover the "lost relation," though her failure is social and historical, rather than the result of the fallenness of humanity. The "aeroplanes" carrying the sky-gods ("narrow silver pencils with two pairs of rigid wings, a long pair in front and a short pair behind"; 126) would seem to confirm this sense of failure before history, for although Coetzee is not concerned with the realistic depiction of period, the airplanes are startlingly anachronistic, so that Magda appears "lost to history" in a rather ordinary sense, too, like a prisoner who does not know that the war is over.

The language of "pure meaning" (125) uttered by the sky-gods is a metaphysical discourse reflecting on the insecurity Magda has demonstrated throughout the novel. Here Coetzee reconstructs lines of argument from Hegel and Sartre that deal with the problem of the presence of the subject to itself, the emergence of being-for-itself through separation and negation, and the dialectic of self and Other. Having been spoken to out of the sky, Magda—to the very end seeking transfiguration through recognition—speaks back, first by shouting skyward and then by placing stones on the veld. "ES MI," she appeals; "VENE!" (130). Later, fearing that the sky-gods will disregard her, treating her as one of the ugly sisters instead of Cinderella herself, she writes, "CINDRLA ES MI" (132). Apprehensive about the gods' superior sophistication, she writes cryptic and alluring poems ("POEMAS CREPUSCLRS"; 132), adding a line each day that the airplanes fly, each line implying invitation, reassurance, or conciliation. In the end, in pure frustration, she resorts to vulgar come-ons; transcendence, in whatever form, proves to be unavailable: "We are the castaways of God as we are the castaways of history," she says finally (135).

In the closing paragraphs Magda returns to her father's side and falls momentarily into a mode of nostalgia in which she constructs the full life she has in fact been unable to achieve for herself. It is a moment of painful bad faith, but Coetzee does not leave Magda in this condition; instead, he allows her to articulate some of the formal and generic conditions that have made her what she is. She imagines herself in another life, in a domestic metropolitan novel, where she might have made up for "physical shortcomings" with "ten nimble fingers on the pianoforte keys and an album full of sonnets" (138). Realizing that the novel of class relations and marriage markets was never available to her, she asks what kind of literature is it that speaks of life on "a barbarous frontier," "in a district outside the law, where the bar against incest is often down, where we pass our days in savage torpor?" (138) One possible answer, she muses, is a pastoral literature in which there are poems about "Verlore Vlakte, about the melancholy of the sunset over the koppies, the sheep beginning to huddle against the first evening chill, the faraway boom of the windmill, the first chirrup of the first cricket" (138). Magda acknowledges that she is not immune to the pastoral idyll but declares finally that she is content to have "uttered my life in my own voice throughout," to have "chosen at every moment her own destiny" (138).

It is not entirely true that she has done so, since, as we have seen, historical processes overwhelm her, but in contrast to the literature of pastoralism in which the alienation and insecurity of the settler are soothed, Magda has certainly explored and revealed the moral and social texture of her situation. Her particular gift has been her transgressiveness, which leaves its outline over social conventions and lines of division; but to that one might add her gift of negativity, her refusal to be seduced by the attractions of losing oneself to the dream of being simply present to oneself and one's history. I have chosen, she says,

> to die here in the petrified garden, behind locked gates, near my father's bones, in a space echoing with hymns I could have written but did not because (I thought) it was too easy. (138)

THREE

Reading the Signs of History

Waiting for the Barbarians

Waiting for the Barbarians is a pivotal work in the development of Coetzee's oeuvre. There are sharp stylistic and narratological differences between *Dusklands* and *In the Heart of the Country,* on the one hand, and *Waiting for the Barbarians,* on the other. These differences include a less experimental treatment of narrative voice, in which conventionality is treated as given rather than displayed with antirealist effects; an emphasis on making "natural" description, despite the absence of historical specificity in the locale; and a highly ordered sense of time, with the narrative being organized around a single seasonal cycle. Clearly, a process of formal stabilization is at work here. The shift cannot be called a return to realism; indeed, if anything, it represents the achievement of a certain self-assurance by Coetzee, who seems to have exorcised at last the ghost of realism.[1] The questions are, How can these developments be related to the concerns addressed in the novel? and In what sense can one speak of these concerns as pivotal?

Waiting for the Barbarians locates itself strategically within that portentous moment of suspension when an increasingly defensive imperialism begins making plans for a final reckoning with its enemies. *Barbarians* is therefore a kind of "interregnum" novel: published in 1980, a year before Gordimer's *July's People,* it shares with the latter work, as Stephen Clingman puts it, the "semiotic" project of "seeing the present through the eyes of the future," in other words, of "decoding the signs and codes of the present" through the perspectives made possible by imagining the future (*Novels of Nadine Gordimer* 202). Of course, it is only in *Life and Times of Michael K* that Coetzee develops a scenario of what looks like revolution; at this stage Coetzee is not projecting a future so much as examining the present as it is lived by many of those who anticipate its imminent collapse. But whereas Gordimer, through future projection, challenges apartheid's system of meanings within the scope provided largely by language and characterization in realist discourse, Coetzee conducts his critique in terms of the basic elements of narrative construction. The semiotic thrust of *Barbarians* is effected, at its most fundamental levels, through the displacement of milieu and the withholding of resolutions, both thematic and narratological.

In the poem by C. P. Cavafy of the same title as the novel, the barbarians enable the Empire to array its forces, reconstitute its hierarchies, display its symbols—in short, to refurbish itself as a complete political and semiotic system. When, in the poem, the enemy does not materialize at the city gates, the Empire's nervous pleasures of anticipation quickly lead to confusion and despondency: "And now what will become of us without Barbarians?— / Those people were some sort of solution" (*Collected Poems* 17–18). Similarly, in the novel there is no conflagration beyond the moment of waiting, with the effect that Coetzee interrupts and suspends the teleology of the colonial state; by showing that Empire's images of the barbarians are wholly contingent on its own need for self-realization, he breaks open the enclosed world of signs on which Empire depends. (Coetzee drops the definite article from "Empire," thus drawing attention to the universalizing forms of self-representation underlying imperialist endeavors.)

It is not that the barbarians are the purely fictive construct of Empire: fictive constructs do not return imperial horsemen strapped dead on their mounts, as a warning (140). What is at issue is how Empire *imagines* the barbarians, and in this respect, against the Empire's certainties, the novel repeatedly counterposes arbitrariness and indeterminacy. There is something deconstructive about this form of critique, but I suggest that in a formal sense it is more accurate to say that the novel works on the basis of what Frank Kermode in *The Sense of an Ending* called *peripeteia*, that is, "the equivalent, in narrative, of irony in rhetoric," where naive expectations of closure are disconfirmed, leading to more complex, if unresolved, versions of "truth" (18).[2]

Waiting for the Barbarians is pivotal, however, not because it deals with a pivotal historical moment, nor because it strategically "freezes" an imperial teleology in order to undermine it; it is pivotal in the sense that for the first time in the sequence of novels, history emerges not as the a priori structure that it tends to be in *Dusklands* and *In the Heart of the Country* but as an object in itself—that is, as a discursive field. It is true that positivist conceptions of history are already rendered problematic in the early fiction. Nevertheless, in *Dusklands* history is the "eveninglands" of the present, the inevitable phase of decolonization against which the penetrative, dominating, and rationalistic projects of colonialism are measured; in *Heart of the Country*, similarly, history is the process that steadily breaks through the "eternal present" of Magda's consciousness, inducing panic and a sense of failure and pushing Magda into desperate attempts to create a transcendent, ahistorical language. In *Barbarians*, by contrast, history becomes objectified as History—thus emerging, in Kermode's terms, as the time of crisis, or *kairos*, as against the time of the seasons, or *chronos* (48). As History, or history-as-myth, history is the peculiar, informing narrative of Empire itself, partly constituting and partly legitimizing Empire's terrorism:

> What has made it impossible for us to live in time like fish in water, like birds in air, like children? It is the fault of Empire! Empire has created the time of history. Empire has located its existence not in the smooth recurrent spinning time of the cycle of the seasons but in the jagged time of rise and fall, of beginning and end, of catastrophe. Empire dooms itself to live in history and plot against history. (133)

So the history that was presented in the first two novels as an absolute horizon to consciousness is here shown primarily as a structure of ideas, and one that has *failed*, moreover, to transform the terms of discourse. Whereas in the first two novels narrative closure was coextensive with what emerges in an uncomplicated way as the historical process itself, in this novel such closure is not allowed, and history becomes little more than an ideological resource, and a *demystified* element, in the hands of Empire. And what we might stubbornly continue to call the historical process cannot now be figured at all—at least *not in terms of what is currently known.*

This last qualification is an important one that will have to be developed, but for the moment it is more important to establish the significance of the turn of events one witnesses in *Barbarians*. The objectification of history-as-myth is the fulcrum, I believe, on which the corpus of six novels rests. After this point, in *Michael K* Coetzee discovers a form of freedom which can be symbolically opposed to the corrosive effects of History; such freedom is found within the practice of writing. A more skeptical treatment of this question emerges in *Foe*, in which authorship is explored allegorically as a contextually constrained and contradictory activity whose minor victories are subject to the way in which history—or, more particularly, the situation of authorship—grants or withholds authority. The questions engaged by the later fiction, however, are incipient in *Waiting for the Barbarians*, in its objectification and demystification of History and in its cautious and nuanced approach to problems of historical consciousness. The process of formal stabilization referred to earlier can be explained, therefore, with reference to this turning of the tables, because it enables Coetzee to obtain a measure of stylistic control over the sweeping claims of historical consciousness that haunt the early fiction, not to mention the culture as a whole.

TOTAL STRATEGY

Readers of *Waiting for the Barbarians* frequently take the novel's non-specific milieu to suggest a form of ethical universalism. There is a difference, however, between universalism—which implies a humanist conception of a transcendent moral consciousness—and a strategic refusal of specificity, a refusal that is the result of being painfully conscious of one's immediate historical location. The milieu of *Barbarians* is the result, I believe, of just such a refusal. What conditions in South Africa in the late 1970s prompted this gesture?

In these years the South African government produced a number of initiatives designed to cope with unique pressures. Internally, a large, unregulated and unruly labor movement had been growing since the early years of the decade; a continuing recession exacerbated unemployment; above all, there was the Soweto Revolt of 1976. Externally, the demise of the Portuguese government in Lisbon in 1974 led to the collapse of its colonies, Mozambique and Angola, where protracted guerrilla wars had been fought for some time near South Africa's borders. The period also saw the intensification of civil war in Zimbabwe, leading to independence by 1980. In response to what it saw as a series of unprecedented threats, the government created commissions of inquiry, charged with investigating the regularization of trade unions, and Party think tanks, designed to devise a racially co-optive constitution; in October 1977 it banned a number of political organizations and individuals, notably those espousing Black Consciousness; it tried to extend middle-class entrepreneurship to blacks, who would serve as a buffer against "communism"; and it refined its elaborate and already totalitarian security apparatus. The central emphases of policy at this time were therefore managerial, technocratic, anticommunist, and military. The umbrella concept linking all of these policies—defined as a response to what was called the "total onslaught"—was "total strategy" (Norval 51–53; Posel 1–4).

Coetzee's Empire is recognizable partly as the fictionalization of this especially paranoid moment in apartheid discourse. In this way, what Rosemary Jane Jolly calls the novel's "territorial metaphor" becomes a form of obliquely referenced political critique. Certainly, Coetzee's Empire represents a continuation of the frontier hypothesis in colonial thinking since the eighteenth century, but specific features connect it to the South Africa of the period when the novel was being written. Indeed, its very remoteness, its deliberate anachronisms, and its denial of historical plausibility resonate with the somewhat phantasmagoric quality of the state's projections and vocabulary at this time. Moreover, the arrival at the Magistrate's outpost of the Third Bureau, led by Colonel Joll, marks the point where the State shifts gear and becomes more blatantly terroristic. As Jean-Philipe Wade points out, there are distinct similarities between explanations given by Colonel Joll for the death of a prisoner in custody (6) and accounts given of the death of Stephen Biko by security policemen at the subsequent inquest ("The Allegorical Text and History" 281). Biko's death in 1977 highlighted the role of torture and detention in the context of a security-dominated state, and the novel's response to these developments is in fact remarkably direct given Coetzee's nonreferential commitments.

If some of the terms on which the fictional Empire is created are taken from current features of South African public life, others, by contrast, are derived from different, far less topical, sources. In three of Coetzee's linguistic essays produced at the time of or shortly after *Waiting for the Barbarians*, extensive reference is made to eighteenth-century prose, notably Defoe, Swift, Newton, and Gibbon.[3] Coetzee's interest in eighteenth-century prose later developed into *Foe*, which is, among other things, a respectful parody of Defoe, but what concerns us here is the nonfictional prose, and especially Gibbon's *Decline and Fall*. These essays have, as their point of origin, stylistic analyses done by Richard Ohmann on Gibbon. Coetzee was interested in the rhetorical effects of passive constructions, which are characteristic of eighteenth-century English prose. Certain elements of the passive style—such as its air of circumspection and the idea of agentlessness—may have provided part of the background for the novel's concern with indeterminacy. But it is equally possible that eighteenth-century historiography provided the essential distinction between civilization and barbarism used by Coetzee—and no doubt by Cavafy before him, for different purposes and in another context—in his fictive displacement of the dominant forms of contemporary South African thinking.

According to François Furet, the historian of the French Revolution, Enlightenment historiography, using classical sources, developed the classification "savage-barbarian-civilized" as a way of distinguishing among the ancients and their competitors. In this schema, whereas savages were simply outside of history altogether, barbarians were a step ahead because they obeyed authority, owned property, used writing materials, and domesticated animals (145–46). The specific notion of the "barbarian" is not well established in the South African racial lexicon (though it does appear in the writings of the eighteenth-century explorer François Le Vaillant). But the eighteenth-century vocabulary is useful for a novel written in the South Africa of the late 1970s, where it was quite natural in official discourse to speak of "nations"—that is, "mature" (i.e., barbarian) black nations—which could be allowed to develop as independent states in their own segregated bantustans, in contrast to a white (civilized) nation, which could be left to its own devices. Such ideas, characteristic of the phase of "separate development" that lasted throughout the period, were a refinement of the earlier, more overtly racist language of apartheid.[4]

In their use of these categories the eighteenth-century historians exploited the ironies that arose from a society's slipping from one state of civilization to another. Citing Diderot, Furet points out that the distinction between a condition of barbarism, on the one hand, and a policed form of civilization, on the other, was rather unclear. Gibbon himself, says Furet, preferred pre-Christian civilization in Rome to Christianized barbarism (146). Such historiographical irony was suggestive in the South African context, where it was reasonable to ask such questions as, Who are the real barbarians, anyway? Thus the Magistrate steels himself to rebel against public torture by saying that the future should be left at least "one man who in his heart was not a barbarian" (104).

Gibbon concludes *Decline and Fall* by saying that it was among the ruins of the Capitol that he first conceived the idea of writing his history. Like earlier historians, he was both moved by the spectacle of the past that reared up from the ruins and struck by the ignorance and superstition of later generations of Romans (685–81). Thus, Hayden White

refers to *Decline and Fall* as "the greatest achievement of sustained
Irony in the history of historical literature" (55). In *Waiting for the
Barbarians* the Magistrate is himself an antiquarian who struggles with
the idea of writing a history of settlement and who spends much time in
the ruins of a former barbarian town in his corner of the Empire's
western provinces, uncovering artifacts and collecting poplar slips containing a script he is trying to decipher. The indecipherability of the slips
and the wholly strategic "reading" the Magistrate gives of them when
called to account for his actions by the agents of the Third Bureau
(110–12) place Coetzee's handling of these questions squarely within
postmodern times, but the connection does suggest that the novel might
owe not only some of its essential vocabulary but also aspects of the
narrative situation to Gibbon's eighteenth-century classic.[5]

THE WRITING OF HISTORY

Whereas Gibbon was able to make the historical record amenable to
ironic manipulation, the Magistrate in *Waiting for the Barbarians,* in his
attempt to write a history of settlement, gets no further than repeating
some of the disingenuous formulas of colonial pastoralism:

> "No one who paid a visit to this oasis," I write, "failed to be struck by the
> charm of life here. We lived in the time of the seasons, of the harvests, of the
> migrations of the waterbirds. We lived with nothing between us and the stars.
> We would have made any concession, had we only known what, to go on
> living here. This was paradise on earth." (154)

He quickly abandons the project, however, describing this beginning as
a "plea" for forgiveness and conciliation; its implicit evasion of the
brutality of imperialism is a trace of the critique of settler-colonial
pastoralism in the earlier fiction. Thus, the Magistrate continues, "It
would be disappointing to know that the poplar slips I have spent so
much time on contain a message as devious, as equivocal, as reprehensi-
ble as this" (154). The Magistrate then makes several efforts at perora-
tion, but a sense of unreality pervades each attempt. The last statement,
which simply expresses the frustration of irresolution, is actually most
convincing: "I think: 'There has been something staring me in the face,
and still I do not see it'" (155).

What is staring him in the face is at one level simply his inability to
produce significant closure, but at another level it is history itself,
history as something brute, impenetrable, and ultimately unrepresent-

able, something that will not be possessed by his efforts to produce a historical discourse. Although he is prepared to imagine that the barbarians of the former settlement might have possessed a code in which it was possible to write history, he discovers that he does not possess such a code himself. What is true of his efforts to write a history of settlement is true also of his antiquarian interests, that is, his excavations, his fascination with the poplar slips, and his night's vigil spent in the ruins trying to conjure an image of the barbarian way of life. Although the outpost in the provinces produces the need, as he puts it, "to find in the vacuousness of the desert a special historical poignancy" (17), his efforts lead nowhere. Kermode is helpful, once again, in explaining the Magistrate's predicament: one of the functions of history is to produce a "concord-fiction," a sense of consonance between past, present, and future; in these terms, history is a kind of substitute for authority and tradition (56). In his isolation from the capital, the Magistrate's historical interests are a series of wistful projects aimed at achieving such consonance. But concord-fictions do not, will not materialize: he remains outside of history, outside, that is, of the *writing-of-history*.

The Magistrate's problem, his inability to achieve an image of continuity from the archaeological remains of the barbarians and their forebears, is addressed in general terms in Foucault's introduction to *The Archeology of Knowledge*. (In presenting the Magistrate's diggings, Coetzee might well have borrowed Foucault's metaphor.) The first consequence of the discovery of discontinuity in contemporary historiography is what Foucault calls "the questioning of the document" (6). Instead of historical data constituting a simple repository of memory from which documents are drawn, tested for their truth-value, and then revealed, history now "organizes the document, divides it up, distributes it, orders it, arranges it in levels, establishes series, distinguishes between what is relevant and what is not, discovers elements, defines unities, describes relations" (6–7). The poplar slips, which the Magistrate tries to read by arranging them in different combinations and patterns (16), foreground this new, enigmatic status of the resources of historical knowledge. Indeed, when the Magistrate "interprets" the slips to Joll, he is not only producing a plausible defense of an imaginary barbarian viewpoint but also asserting the open-endedness of the script. The slips, he says, form an allegory, offering different orders of meaning that, like the cries of the dead, are open to many interpretations (112). Even this use of the slips, however, which opposes pre- and post-Saussurean conceptions of language in an allegory of the indeterminacy of signification, is a strategic one, for it is aimed at undermining Joll's terroristic drive for certainty, for truth. If the writing of history is a substitute for authority and tradition, then the Magistrate's interpretation of the slips is a momentary but significant rejection of the authority of Joll and of the tradition of Empire.[6] This is the Magistrate's own "organization of the document," to use Foucauldian terminology. But although he is able to put the slips to use in this way, the Magistrate has still not solved the problem of transforming the "empty signifiers" of history into coherent forms of historical consciousness.

THE SUBJECT OF HISTORY

The problem of the writing of history is part of a larger inquiry in the novel that has to do with contextual pressures on the general process of signification. Semiosis, subjectivity, and the moral ideal of a human community are intimately linked in *Barbarians*. Implicit in the need for historical continuity is the need to preserve the sovereignty and transcendence of the subject. Foucault makes this need explicit: historical continuity is both a "guarantee that everything that has eluded [the subject] may be restored" and a promise "that one day the subject—in the form of historical consciousness—will once again be able to appropriate, to bring back under his sway, all those things that are kept at a distance by difference" (*Archeology of Knowledge* 12).

Foucault's "difference" opens up for us the Magistrate's relationship with the unnamed girl who, with several others, is captured and tortured by Joll to obtain information about barbarian intentions. His desire, in this relationship, has to do precisely with the girl's difference, with what he calls at one point her "old free state" (34); possession of this difference would consolidate the Magistrate's subject-position. The Hegelian allegory of master and slave, familiar from the early fiction, is applicable here, but in this context what is striking is a direct analogy between the form of subject-constitution implicit in the desire for historical continuity and the form of subject-constitution promised by the relationship with the girl. Indeed, these elements—manifested as reading the poplar slips, on the one hand, and knowing how the girl's body came to be marked, on the other—are explicitly linked: "It has been growing more and more clear to me that until the marks on this girl's body are deciphered and understood I cannot let go of her" (31).

Despite his obsessive attentions, however, the Magistrate is unable to lead the relationship to any kind of reciprocal intimacy. From his point of view, there is no direction and no penetration: "These bodies of hers and mine are diffuse, gaseous, centreless, at one moment spinning about a vortex here, at another curdling, thickening elsewhere; . . . I know what to do with her no more than one cloud in the sky knows what to do with another" (34). Their encounters usually lead him to oblivious sleep, "like death to me, or enchantment, blank, outside time" (31). By contrast, the Magistrate's exploits with the "little bird-woman" at the inn are penetrative and climactic (though mutually dissembling as well). The contrast between the two relationships is, of course, the point of interest: in a strictly semiotic sense, it represents the difference between what Roland Barthes called the writerly and readerly texts (S/Z 4).[7] (The "bird-woman" is readerly, giving herself over to the agency of the Magistrate; the barbarian girl is writerly, admitting no access to an imagined, fecund essence.) So the barbarian girl will simply not be delivered up to the Magistrate's probings; her otherness cannot be domesticated. The connection between this lack of reciprocity and the Magistrate's inability to create an image of historical continuity is developed further when he speaks of her effect on him in terms of an experience of ahistoricity and atemporality: "I am the same man I always was; but time has broken, something has fallen in upon me from the sky, at random, from nowhere: this body in my bed, for which I am responsible, or so it seems, otherwise why do I keep it?" (43).

The girl is an enigmatic presence, then, thwarting the process of subject-constitution. She is also, however, more multivalent than the foregoing analysis might suggest. At the most obvious level, she represents a continuation of the longing for community that we have encountered before, in Magda in *In the Heart of the Country*. But whereas in Magda's case female desire for belonging and association can be read as the desire to escape from the loneliness that attends the colonizing history of the male father, the Magistrate's desire in *Barbarians* brings in train all the dominating implications of the colonial episteme. The desired, female colonized is well known as a trope of colonial discourse, whether she represents the interior and its material riches, the landscape, or the purely psychic abundance of the unknown. In disallowing penetration, therefore, Coetzee both acknowledges and refuses to perpetuate these generalized implications of dominance.

There are other, more specific implications. The girl's mystery is partly the result of torture.[8] Foucault argues in *Discipline and Punish* that the purpose of torture is to get to the soul, the last vestige of selfhood in which resistance lies buried. As such, torture is in fact a way

of *producing* the soul, for it writes soulhood on the body through pain
(29). To put it another way, individuality is signified, constructed,
precisely in order that it may be destroyed; similarly, "pain is truth,"
says the Magistrate in *Barbarians*, paraphrasing Joll (5). Later, after
being tortured himself, the Magistrate uses language similar to
Foucault's: "He [Mandel] deals with my soul: every day he folds the
flesh aside and exposes my soul to the light" (118). At this early stage,
then, the torture marks on the girl are signifiers pointing the Magistrate
toward her individuality.[9]

Tortured as she is, the Magistrate's attentions, which involve washing
her feet, take the basic form of atonement or expiation. This is a further
significant implication, introducing the novel's parodic link with the
moral framework of South African liberal humanism. The washing of
feet invokes this context, placing the emphasis on liberalism's Christian
component—a nuance that brings to mind, most obviously, the figure of
Alan Paton. The liberal Christian path to social justice through forgiveness and reconciliation has as its literary correlative the religious tragedy
of *Cry, the Beloved Country*. Coetzee's emphasis is to provide a gentle
critique of this heritage, a critique that repoliticizes and eroticizes it,
displaying liberalism's fetishization of victimhood and revealing it as a
more humane but still essentially self-validating and dominating form of
"soul-formation."[10] Thus, looking at the image of himself in the partially
blinded eyes of the girl, the Magistrate begins to see the image of Joll:

> I am disquieted. "What do I have to do to move you?" . . . "Does no one
> move you?"; and with a shift of horror I behold the answer that has been
> waiting all the time offer itself to me in the image of a face masked by two
> black glassy insect eyes from which there comes no reciprocal gaze but only
> my doubled image cast back at me. . . . *No! No! No!* . . . There is nothing to
> link me with torturers. (44)

The realization of complicity proves to be intolerable for the Magistrate.
He tries to forget the girl by paying more frequent visits to the bird-
woman, but without effect. Gradually, the conviction grows that he
should undertake a journey to the barbarians to restore the girl to her
people.

A powerful contributory factor in this decision is his recurring dream
in which he sees children building a fort of snow in the middle of a wide
plain. The dreams crystallize in lucid imagery the meaning of his desires
for continuity and reciprocity. In their play the children copy the form of
life the Magistrate knows: they are building a castle, analogous to the

Magistrate's outpost. The central image is that of a young girl who sits hooded with her back toward the advancing Magistrate. At first he is unable to imagine her face (10); later, he peers around and sees a face "blank, featureless; it is the face of an embryo or a tiny whale; it is not a face at all but another part of the human body" (37). In the next dream, fearing disappointment, he looks at her again, but this time he sees that "she is herself, herself as I have never seen her, a smiling child, the light sparkling on her teeth and glancing from her jet black eyes" (53). The implications are clear: through the sequence of dreams, the child acquires greater definition, offering herself as an achieved individuality, a process that contrasts directly with the Magistrate's experience in relation to the captured girl. The dreams are not entirely a form of wish fulfillment, however, for the fort of snow that the children are making is uninhabited. The Magistrate draws attention to this omission, but the children carry on as before. "Night after night," he says, "I return to the waste of the snowswept square, trudging towards the figure at its centre, reconfirming each time that the town she is building is empty of life" (53). Both continuity and reciprocity, the two great sites of lack in the Magistrate's discourse thus far, ultimately depend on the idea of human community. This absence stands out poignantly in the dream sequence, providing an important part of the preparation for the expedition.

Broadly, then, the Magistrate's broken subjectivity teaches by extreme example what it means to live in the world of Empire, in Joll's world. This is, I suggest, the logical end reached by the semiotic disarrangement effected on the imperial teleology in the first three parts of the novel. Coetzee's concern with the general question of signification is to treat it as a point of disintegration in the historical situation of imperial violence. The forms of closure demanded by Empire and by Joll are not only arbitrary and terroristic impositions; they are also destructive of coherent forms of life. Outside of community, the various elements simply cannot be brought together. Thus, the semiotic and ethical aspects of Coetzee's analysis are mutually reinforcing.

Ironically, and appropriately, the Magistrate's relationship with the barbarian girl is consummated during the expedition to return her—that is, just as he is about to lose her. Having reached the mountains, faced with a party of barbarian soldiers—staring into the muzzle of the leader's rifle—he offers her the choice of returning with him to the settlement. Naturally, she declines (70–71). It is only *outside* the limits of Empire that he can present her with a free choice, but she knows that this freedom would be undermined the minute she accepts. It would be

too easy to read the expedition as a ploy to win the girl again by
momentarily restoring her freedom. He is less calculating, less in control, and the journey is more hazardous than such a reading would
imply. The expedition is the central narrative movement of the whole
novel; after it, the Magistrate's opposition to Joll is sealed, and he is
imprisoned and tortured. It is therefore an act of significant choice,
analogous to Magda's parricides in *Heart of the Country*: it involves an
attempt to reject the subjective space that his circumstances and history
have prepared for him. When the Magistrate recalls, some time after the
expedition, that for the girl he and Joll merely represented "two sides of
imperial rule," with himself the emblem of "the lie that Empire tells
itself when times are easy" and Joll "the truth that Empire tells when
harsh winds blow" (135), he is trying to put as much distance as possible
between himself and the self of imperialism.

RESISTANCE FROM WITHIN

The question then arises, if the Magistrate is trying to abandon the
subject-position of Empire, *where can he go?* Apart from the fact that
subject-positions are not freely chosen, we cannot expect the Magistrate,
as the autodiegetic narrator of a discourse located *within* the epistemological framework of colonialism, to try to discover or position himself
within a putative *barbarian* subjectivity. Indeed, it is intrinsic to the
critique of Empire in the novel that a barbarian subject-position remains
unrepresented; the girl's enigmatic qualities, in particular, block the
course of the Magistrate's unusual but nevertheless predatory intentions. The novel's position on this question is close to that formulated
more recently by Gayatri Chakravorty Spivak: "No perspective *critical*
of imperialism can turn the Other into a self, because the project of
imperialism has always already historically refracted what might have
been the absolutely Other into a domesticated Other that consolidates
the imperialist self" ("Three Women's Texts" 253). Spivak presents this
argument categorically, but we should not insist on its general applica-
bility in all imperialist accounts of the Other. Coetzee's Empire will not
stand for all empires; its critical force is to provide a strategic, timely
disconfirmation.

In the second half of *Barbarians* (parts 4–6) several paths are opened
to the Magistrate in relation to narrative developments. In each case the
position he articulates is rooted *in* the dominating framework, even

though a struggle is being conducted there. The first of these positions amounts to a temporary retreat into an amoral existentialism when he is placed under pressure. While the army under the command of the Third Bureau undertakes a new campaign, a prison is erected in the town, what Coetzee calls, with reference to Hawthorne's *The Scarlet Letter*, the "black flower of civilization" (79). After feeling elated, momentarily, that the "bond" with Empire is broken, that he is "a free man," the Magistrate quickly learns through confinement, humiliation, and torture the simple existential truth that the body sets clear limits to what can be endured or claimed on behalf of ideas or principles. The freedoms he begins to value most are the simple, elemental ones: "To lie in a woman's arms in a proper bed, to have good food to eat, to walk in the sun—how much more important these seem than the right to decide without advice from the police who should be my friends and who my enemies!" (96). Although this position is typically compromised, he is rewarded in the dreams with an image in which he nurtures the injured girl (87); later she appears as a fairy-tale princess in a dark blue robe, her hair gold-braided; she rewards him for his pain with freshly baked bread in a sacramental gesture of conciliation (109). The culmination of this trend comes in the final dream, when, blown by the wind, they collide: "For an instant I have a vision of her face, the face of a child, glowing, healthy, smiling on me without alarm" (136). Reciprocation comes, therefore, after the Magistrate has felt something of the suffering experienced by the girl, but only in the muted form implied by its displacement to dream life.

But this is not a final position. When the Magistrate witnesses the public torture of a new group of barbarians by Joll after the return of the army, he is reminded of the first round of interrogations, of the girl especially, and is moved to mount a certain resistance once again—particularly when a hammer is drawn out for the purpose of breaking the prisoners' feet, a fate suffered by the girl. At this point he expresses old-fashioned, liberal values of decency. Coetzee's literary precedent would appear to be Kafka's "In the Penal Colony"—notably in Joll's writing "ENEMY" on the backs of the prisoners and in the Magistrate's resounding "*No!*" to the spectacle of cruelty. The Magistrate's protestations, though simple and direct, are also inhibited, as if he struggles to voice them in a situation in which they appear out of place, perhaps bookish: "'Look!' I shout. 'We are the great miracle of creation! But from some blows this miraculous body cannot repair itself! How—!' Words fail me. 'Look at these men!' I recommence. '*Men!*'" (107).

The question that surfaces at this point is that of the status of liberal values in a situation that simply has no room for them anymore. The outpost was, of course, always fundamentally illiberal. Thus, the Magistrate remembers lecturing a soldier, without belief, on the rule of law and recalls feeling afterwards "the shame of office" (139). On that occasion, he also tried to console himself by elevating his role to that of the witness to suffering, a role sanctified with an air of tragedy (and pursued, as we have seen, by the literature of liberal dissent in South Africa): "'When some men suffer unjustly,' I said to myself, 'it is the fate of those who witness their suffering to suffer the shame of it.' But the specious consolation of this thought could not comfort me" (139). Under the Magistrate's laissez-faire brand of colonial humanism, liberal values appeared equivocal at best; thus, in the new order they can have even less currency. Indeed, they appear thoroughly anachronistic in Joll's reign, though this fact is also laced with the irony that such values might have a new, interim relevance in the terrorism of the imperial crisis.

The Magistrate's liberalism, however, does not provide a final position either. For one thing, as he acknowledges, it is easier to assert standards of fair play than to call for justice or the surrender of power (108). Indeed, none of the options available to the Magistrate has lasting validity; in fact, it is more typical that events leave him feeling baffled and stupid. The Magistrate does not, and cannot, provide a satisfying resolution, and therefore the position with which he concludes is that of suspension in ignorance, of simply *not knowing* what the future might deliver. Though everyone in the town indulges in "dreams of ends," in "all of us, deep down," as he puts it, "there seems to be something granite and unteachable" (143).

RESISTING HISTORY

Toward the conclusion of the novel the Magistrate conjures with images of imperialism's fierce encounter with its end. The images that come are textbook ones, images of cataclysm and triumph drawn from History's stock-in-trade. The Magistrate reproduces them, toys with them, feels their power, and thereby thinks his way into the symbolic resources of imperialism's crisis. But the fictional elements with which Coetzee contextualizes the Magistrate's consciousness undermine these images in a curious fashion: the impending darkness, the water in which he is wading, calf-deep—these suggest a steady sliding into the unconscious, as if the very imagery of the end-of-history, thrown up by Empire, were itself subject to a dimly recognized process of *Aufhebung*. The Magistrate struggles, as it were, to get *beyond* the moment of the end, ultimately without success, and the result of this movement is a jolt back into the ordinariness of the present:

> One thought alone preoccupies the submerged mind of Empire: how not to end, how not to die, how to prolong its era. By day it pursues its enemies. It is cunning and ruthless, it sends its bloodhounds everywhere. By night it feeds on images of disaster: the sack of cities, the rape of populations, pyramids of bones, acres of desolation. A mad vision yet a virulent one: I, wading in the ooze, am no less infected with it than the faithful Colonel Joll as he tracks the enemies of Empire through the boundless desert, sword unsheathed to cut down barbarian after barbarian until at last he finds and slays the one whose destiny it should be (or if not he then his son's or unborn grandson's) to climb the bronze gateway to the Summer Palace and topple the globe surmounted by the tiger rampant that symbolizes eternal dominion, while his comrades below cheer and fire their muskets in the air.
>
> There is no moon. In darkness I grope my way back to dry land and on a bed of grass, wrapped in my cloak, fall asleep. I wake up stiff and cold from a flurry of confused dreams. The red star has barely moved in the sky. (133–34)

This passage, like many in the closing pages of *Barbarians,* curiously mixes skepticism and renunciation. The skepticism is easy to define: it involves the intuition that every image of the end is, in its own way, an image of the present projected onto the moment of the end. Or to put it more strongly, it involves the conviction that, as Georg Lukács has it, "every definition degenerates into an illusion: *history is the history of the unceasing overthrow of the objective forms that shape the life of man*" (186). Of course, in Lukács what prevents this process from falling into relativism is the developing consciousness of the proletariat; in the Magistrate there is none of this faith. But does this mean that Coetzee himself has abandoned the sense of historical inevitability that accompanies the trajectory of decolonization in the earlier fiction?

At a philosophical level it would be possible to describe the Magistrate's position as irrational and pessimistic rather than optimistic and dialectical: Nietzsche and Spengler rather than Hegel and Marx. But this seems a rather heavy-handed overwriting of the Magistrate's position. What it ignores is his rhetorical situation, indeed, his *historical* situation. The Magistrate's unwillingness to accept the endings projected by Empire, an unwillingness that he presents with a certain self-deprecation as ignorance or stupidity, is a *positional* response to a specific cultural configuration. For the question is ultimately not about the laws of history but about who controls the signs of power. In this sense the Magistrate's attitude is one of renunciation. What is renounced is the large agenda, the need for final conclusions. This is not a nineteenth-century resolution but a contemporary one that is low key and deliberately marginal, though critical; postmodern, but also mindful of the limits faced by historical subjects in their symbolic constructions.

This seems to be the proper perspective from which to regard the fact that the temporal dimension of the narrative, from the moment of Joll's arrival to his abandonment of the outpost to the barbarians, is remarkably orderly, built around a single seasonal cycle. There are, of course, poetic-symbolic correspondences between the seasons and certain narrative events: the activities of the Third Bureau at the beginning of the novel coincide with the start of winter; signs of spring emerge after the expedition to return the girl; and so on. But the whole structure of one year is a flagrantly formal, conventionalized device. Rather than representing an attempt to absorb history into Nature, it represents the deployment of a more restricted truth that can be traced crudely as follows: historical time is a construction imposed on formless chronicity, as part of the work of culture; fiction can *restore* the perspective in which the constructedness of time becomes apparent. *Waiting for the Barbarians* does so by setting two forms of time, *kairos* and *chronos*, in opposition to one another. Its critical effects depend on its ability to *disorganize* historical time. Whereas a realist narrative would depend on the construction of a coherent image of historical time, Coetzee's novel works the other way: it must dissolve such an image, and it does so by setting it in relation to its opposite. Thus, resisting History, the Magistrate tries to imagine himself inhabiting another temporal order: "I lie on the bare mattress and concentrate on bringing into life the image of myself as a swimmer swimming with even, untiring strokes through the medium of time, a medium more inert than water, without ripples, pervasive, colourless, odourless, dry as paper" (143).

Coetzee allows his narrative one ingenuous, symbolic gesture toward the future. In the final scene the Magistrate finds himself approaching a group of children playing in the yard of the barracks, building a snowman. Has the wish fulfillment of the recurring dream become reality? Not quite, for this is "not the scene I dreamed of," and he leaves it without understanding—"like a man who lost his way long ago but presses on along a road that may lead nowhere" (155–56). Nevertheless, what the children produce is "not a bad snowman" (155). Do the children represent a future community, creating the conditions for a reconstructed subject? This is at least a limited possibility, even though the novel has not invested its critical and fictive energies in its definition.

FOUR

Writing in
"the cauldron of history"

Life and Times of Michael K and *Foe*

In his later fiction J. M. Coetzee turns to the situation of writing itself. This is a logical development given that *Waiting for the Barbarians* is concerned with the discursive underpinnings of Empire. As I have shown, *Barbarians* responds to a particular moment in the elaboration of apartheid discourse; similarly, *Life and Times of Michael K* was written partly—with the emphasis on partly—in response to a particular political and constitutional debate in South Africa in the early 1980s, when the nation seemed to enter a cycle of insurrection and repression whose outcome threatened to be bloody. Despite the similarity of reference, in the later fiction (both *Michael K* and *Foe*) Coetzee takes a sharper turn toward discursivity, finding still fewer ready connections between history and representation than he had before. In *Barbarians*, narration follows the course of history into the end of Empire; in the later fiction, by contrast, narration more clearly establishes its own points of departure.

This increased sense of independence goes hand-in-hand with an ability to register even more acutely the scope and limitations of novelistic discourse within a culture obviously in crisis. On this paradox the later fiction turns. Although the scenario of civil war set out in *Michael K* predicts the consequences of current state policies, at a deeper level Coetzee has freed himself from the burden of having to unravel the meaning of the last stage of colonialism, which consensus takes to be immanent in the events of the day. Indeed, a new subject has begun to take over and shape the fiction, namely, the nature of, and the conditions governing, the power to narrate, a power that appears to Coetzee to be more palpable than ever. It is true, of course, that Coetzee has always displayed and questioned novelistic conventions; at this point, though, the possibilities for writing novels within a highly politicized culture, a culture dominated by claims and counterclaims about the meaning of living on a historical cusp, have shifted to center stage. If we follow Coetzee down this path, we might understand the political improbabilities of *Michael K*, a novel about a subject who, miraculously, lives through the trauma of South Africa in a state of civil war without being touched by it; we might also appreciate the contextual sensitivities of *Foe*, a novel that, while apparently rich in postmodern play, is also a skeptical, indeed scrupulous, interrogation of the authority of white South African authorship.

THE TIME OF POLITICS

Coetzee has said that *Life and Times of Michael K* is "about a time when it is too late for politics" ("Too Late for Politics?" 6). Politics, in this sense, is what comes *before* and *after* the revolution; what happens *during* the revolution is the violent release of forces that politics under "normal" circumstances tries either to marshal or to oppose. In Gramscian terms, the wars of movement and position have given way to underground warfare (Gramsci 229). There is literally only one sentence in which politics, in this sense, is "remembered" in the entire text of *Michael K*. It is given to Major Noël van Rensburg, commander of the Kenilworth rehabilitation camp, during the Medical Officer's narration in part 2:

> "Also," I said, "can you remind me why we are fighting this war? I was told once, but that was long ago and I seem to have forgotten."
> "We are fighting this war," Noël said, "so that minorities will have a say in their destinies."
> We exchanged empty looks. Whatever my mood was, I could not get him to share it. (215)

The reason for the Medical Officer's bemusement is that the novel is indeed about a different time, a time when the exigencies of the war itself have superseded the issues that precipitated it. No doubt the Medical Officer's attitude corresponds to a certain weary incredulity on Coetzee's own part regarding the policies and practices of the National party in the early 1980s, but against this ironic note it is important to say that the novel's scenario of militarism and civil attrition challenges the politics of the "destiny of minorities" in South Africa, a politics that was taking itself very seriously at the time. In other words, the social panorama of *Michael K* is presented against the grain of official policy formulation. Of course, opposing the National party is unexceptional, but it is important to note Coetzee's starting point, for the novel's metafictional dimensions could be misconstrued if the element of social critique is not properly acknowledged at the outset. Let me now turn to the context in which this critique is developed.

Life and Times of Michael K was published in 1983. Between the elections of 1981 and 1984, white South African politics was dominated by a debate about "multinationalism." These years included a referendum called to approve the National party's new constitutional proposals, perhaps the most important feature of its movement toward limited reform. Under the bonapartist leadership of P. W. Botha, the government undertook the unlikely task of "broadening the base of democracy" without jeopardizing the white minority's authority and interests. Its emphasis on multinationalism was calculated to legitimize this process. Some of the key aspects of this thinking had been adumbrated in Botha's "twelve point plan" of 1979, which began with the assertion that there had to be an "acknowledgment and acceptance of multinationalism and minorities in South Africa" (South African Institute of Race Relations 10). The new constitution, inaugurated in 1984, replaced a single white parliament with a tricameral system of three houses for whites, "coloreds," and Indians, theoretically bringing the "minorities" into an alliance in matters of common interest. Needless to say, the black majority was excluded from the system altogether, since its interests were supposedly taken care of in the policy of national independence for the bantustans.

For the present purposes, the most remarkable aspect of this development was the government's apparent belief that it could create and impose a constitution aimed at achieving greater legitimacy without taking into account the objections of black leaders of almost every constituency, including not only the ANC and its internal affiliates but also homeland leaders and party representatives of the very "colored" and Indian groups the system was designed to co-opt. The whole project became a charade, undertaken, as Alf Stadler comments, "in the absence of any effort to address the key issues in South Africa's current crisis: the absence of common political rights at the national level, the racial basis of existing rights, and the authoritarian controls over political organization and action" (171). Stadler's point goes to the heart of the sense of arbitrariness that the idea of politics accrues in *Michael K*: the novel exploits the unreality of the state's efforts at constitutional reform; this is the force of the Medical Officer's confusion in the foregoing quotation.

More grimly, though, in its projections of civil war *Michael K* shows the *consequences* of the state's spectacular failure to address the essentials of the crisis it was facing. The scenario is not strictly apocalyptic; rather, it anticipates accelerated militarization in response to sporadic but growing insurrection and guerrilla activity. Coetzee's South Africa of the near future is a society of nightly curfews; restrictions on movement between districts; labor, resettlement, rehabilitation, and internment camps (with reclassification up the scale as the situation worsens); squatting by the destitute and demolition of abandoned buildings by the state; armored patrols and protected civilian convoys; widespread lawlessness, including looting by the poor and corruption on the part of the rich; failing economic markets replaced by production quotas; and, last, a dual currency, with one currency passing into obsolescence. In sociopolitical terms, it is a finely drawn and sophisticated picture. And although one acknowledges that prediction per se is not the primary concern of future projection—as Stephen Clingman puts it, the point of this kind of fiction is rather to analyze the hidden propensities of the *present* from the perspective of an *imagined* future (*Novels of Nadine Gordimer*)—after the States of Emergency of 1985–1990, with their mass mobilization campaigns, repression, and deep economic crises, it is hard to resist the observation that *Life and Times of Michael K* stands as perhaps the most accurate of several attempts in South African fiction of the period at giving concrete shape to an imagined future.[1]

THE POLITICS OF ELUSION

"To my ear," says Coetzee, "'The Life' implies that the life is over, whereas 'Life' does not commit itself" ("Two Interviews" 454). We traduce the purposes of *Life and Times of Michael K* if we make claims for either its political percipience or its predictive power without substantially refining the argument. Its intensity lies not in social representation but in the creation of a protagonist of extraordinary symbolic power who becomes, in turn, the focus of a struggle for control over the resources of fictionality itself. Although it would be eminently possible to find his analogue in Cape Town, in a sector of the ragged, homeless, and largely apolitical underclass of the streets, Michael K is not a historical being at all. In this respect, Coetzee carries something over from the first two novels: as he points out in an interview with Stephen Watson, Jacobus Coetzee is and is not an eighteenth-century frontiersman; Magda is and is not a nineteenth-century colonial spinster (Coetzee, "Speaking"). As the Medical Officer says, Michael K is "the obscurest of the obscure, so obscure as to be a prodigy" (195). It is because he is prodigious that a metafictional contest is staged over what K means. To the last, however, K remains his own person: in refusing to be imprisoned in any way, either in the literal camps or in the nets of meaning cast by those who follow after him, he becomes—in the socially symbolic field of the novel's engagement with South Africa, that is, in the field of reading and interpretation—a principle of limited, provisional freedom, a freedom located in the act of writing. However, before consolidating my own hermeneutic capture of Michael K, I must take account of what is at stake in this contest—for the novel does inscribe interpretation as a *contest* and an exercise in power.

On publication, *Michael K* aroused a fair amount of controversy, some of which appeared in the pages of the *African Communist* in a review entitled "Much Ado about Nobody," which appeared shortly after the announcement that the novel had won the Booker-McConnell Prize. The reviewer (identified only as "Z. N.") passes through degrees of irritation before finally dismissing Coetzee's novel: "The absence of any meaningful relationship between Michael K and anybody else . . . means that in fact we are dealing not with a human spirit but an amoeba, from whose life we can draw neither example nor warning because it is too far removed from the norm, unnatural, almost inhuman. Certainly those interested in understanding or transforming South African society can learn little from the life and times of Michael K" (103). Nadine Gordimer's review in the *New York Review of Books* is less dismissive, but the criticism is much the same: a "revulsion against all political and revolutionary solutions rises with the insistence of the song of cicadas to the climax of this novel." She adds that although "what human beings do to fellow human beings" is fully depicted in *Michael K*—and "could not be better said"—nevertheless Coetzee "does not recognize what the victims, seeing themselves as victims no longer, have done, are doing, and believe they must do for themselves" ("Idea of Gardening" 6).

Stephen Clingman, in an essay that contrasts *Michael K* with Gordimer's *July's People* and Serote's *To Every Birth Its Blood*, comments on what he calls the novel's "outright rejections," asking, "Are they not fundamentally evasive and conservative?" ("Revolution and Reality" 48). Clingman cautiously proposes several "defences" of Coetzee, however. One defense relies on Fernand Braudel in suggesting that Coetzee might be taken to support the notion of "the *long durée* of a history of frames of consciousness"; another argues that Coetzee might be advocating a "principled 'negative' dialectic" that rejects both the colonial power, as the dominant term, and its antithesis, thus keeping open the possibilities for some as yet unimaginable future moment (49). These hypotheses are intriguing; I certainly share Clingman's sense that Coetzee would prefer not to assume too much about the course of history. What is striking, however, about all three of these positions is their common, undeclared assumption that the limits of fictionality lie in representation. Insofar as Gordimer and Clingman, independently of one another, are prepared to accept that the novel works outside the conventions of realism, they do so to suggest how Coetzee is making political choices through a medium of allegory; what kind of allegory this might be, however, is largely left unexplored. None of these criticisms of *Michael K* ventures a word on the novel's structure or heterodiegetic narration—that is, on the work's metafictional features.

The charge of elusion in *Michael K*, whether stated or implied, is therefore premature. It declines the challenge of the novel's own self-reflection on questions of power and interpretation and exempts itself, moreover, from the force of this questioning. When Coetzee chooses not to represent mass resistance or project, however tentatively, a utopian future, it would be appropriate—because we are dealing with fiction that has always placed the speaking subject in question—to ask whether this decision might not be attributable to Coetzee's sensitivity to the problem of authority within the fractured and unequal context of South African nationhood (in which this and every other South African narrative resides). *Waiting for the Barbarians* does not presume to speak from a position outside the colonial episteme; similarly, the narrator of the first and third sections of *Michael K* chooses to speak from the same position, and as I have argued before, this degree of caution, even sobriety, about historical knowledge is more responsive to history than is sometimes recognized.

FATHER AND MOTHER

Life and Times of Michael K presents us both with the story of K and with a struggle for control over the meaning of that story. The story has an elemental simplicity that lends itself to conventional allegorical reading, although this is not exclusively a political allegory. Michael K, a municipal gardener who spent his childhood in a children's home, undertakes an improbable journey in the middle of a civil war, wheeling his mother in a makeshift cart from Cape Town to Prince Albert in the Karoo. He intends to return her to the farm where she spent part of her youth in a family of servants; she dies en route, but he continues the journey and scatters her ashes at what seems to be the farm. There he discovers the meaning of his vocation as a gardener and plants seeds. Soon debilitated by hunger and exhaustion, he is found and taken to Jakkalsdrif labor camp; he escapes, returns to the farm, replants, and spends a few blessed weeks tending his pumpkins and melons. Guerrillas pass through, but K decides not to join them; he is then captured, accused of supplying the enemy, taken back to Cape Town, and placed in a rehabilitation camp. He escapes again, however, and spends his last days as a vagrant in Sea Point, where his mother had worked as a domestic servant before they left.

Two features of the story appear to carry allegorical weight: K's embrace of the role of gardener and his elusiveness. The two aspects are connected. For example, in the first of the periods spent at the farm, K senses a growing resilience within himself, which he describes in terms of the differences of soil and climate between Wynberg Park in Cape Town and the Karoo: "It is no longer the green and the brown that I want but the yellow and the red; not the wet but the dry; not the dark but the light; not the soft but the hard. I am becoming a different kind of man . . . I am becoming smaller and harder and drier every day" (92). In other words, the discovery that being a gardener is his "nature" contributes directly to K's developing sense of inviolability. But why should *gardening* be given such significance? The answer has to do with the poles of symbolic possibility that K negotiates throughout his journey, a binary opposition between the principles of Father and Mother. K's biological father is scarcely known; the father here is the political father, with its roots in psychoanalysis.[2] It is the father of the camps, of order, and of institutions: "my father was Huis Norenius," he says; he was "the list of rules on the door of the dormitory" (143). The novel's epigraph, drawn from Heraclitus's *Cosmic Fragments*, presents the war, too, as belonging to the domain of the father:

> War is the father of all and king of all.
> Some he shows as gods, others as men.
> Some he makes slaves, and others free.

The idea that war can produce order through strife (Heraclitus, *Fragments*; T. M. Robinson, "Commentary," in *Heraclitus* 118) is curiously close to the Foucauldian notion of power as a force dispersed through every level of social relations, including the production of subjectivity. In *Power/Knowledge* Foucault reverses Clausewitz's definition of war as the continuation of politics by other means. If politics, in terms of this reversal, is the continuation of war by other means, then we are concerned with violent conflict as a pervasive and, indeed, constitutive element in, as Foucault puts it, "social institutions, in economic inequalities, in language, in the bodies themselves of each and everyone of us" (90). *Michael K* is close to the Foucauldian theme but with this important difference: in Foucault, power is not only pervasive but also productive; by contrast, in the novel, although power penetrates through the layered relations of the social and the subjective, it is also much more corrosive. There is much perfunctory violence in *Michael K*, and motifs of appropriation stand out sharply. This quality is especially apparent in Coetzee's repeated use of a metaphor of parasitism to describe fundamental relations: the towns and the camps, the war and those who live through it, are figured frequently in terms of parasite and host. "The state rides on the backs of earth-grubbers like Michaels," says the Medical Officer; "it devours the products of their toil and shits on them in return" (221). In another example, K thinks, "Perhaps in truth whether the camp was declared a parasite on the town or the town a parasite on the camp depended on no more than who made his voice heard loudest" (160).[3]

As the mother opposes the father, gardening is the opposite of this corrosive notion of power. From the moment K leaves Cape Town and travels into the jaws of the war with his mother in the cart, his resistances become associated metonymically with the mother; and when K distributes her ashes like seed and turns them into the soil of the farm, *cultivation* is added to the chain of significance. Simply put, Coetzee exploits the symbolism of mother earth. Critics and reviewers have extended themselves on this symbolism, partly, I am sure, because its very simplicity makes it seem either implausible or suggestive of ever

more alluring depths. Stephen Clingman wonders whether Coetzee is
reading the South African situation in the light of Voltaire's dictum *Il
faut cultiver notre jardin* in *Candide* ("Revolution and Reality" 57n).
Derek Wright sees something Wordsworthian in the earth symbolism,
the Wordsworth of the Leech-Gatherer and the Old Cumberland Beggar
(116). Gordimer is more direct: "Beyond all creeds and moralities, this
work of art asserts, there is only one: to keep the earth alive, and only
one salvation, the survival that comes from her" ("Idea of Gardening"
6). (A feminist objection might be registered to the association of earth
and mother offered in a straightforward symbolic reading.)

In *Countries of the Mind* Dick Penner also allows the symbolism its
full allegorical weight, to the extent of reading the work as an adapta-
tion of the South African farm novel and *plaasroman* (as well as an
exemplum of the American genre of agrarian protest fiction); this is an
intriguing possibility in the light of Coetzee's interest in the genre and in
colonial pastoralism and landscape description more generally, evident
in several of the essays collected in *White Writing*. However, these
discourses are discussed in *White Writing* as part of the ideological
equipment of the colonists in their efforts to establish relationships with
the land based on property and the maintenance of existing social
relations. K is a different kind of creature from the historical subjects
who invest the soil with this kind of significance. This difference is
clearly illustrated in his decision to avoid setting up a "rival line" to the
Visagie's after the return to the farm of the Visagie heir, now a deserter
from the army. The novel therefore projects landed property, and the
ideological configurations ratifying it under colonialism, as belonging to
the domain of the father, not the mother. Hence Coetzee can argue in
White Writing, "If the pastoral writer mythologizes the earth as a
mother, it is more often than not as a harsh, dry mother without curves
or hollows, infertile, unwilling to welcome her children back even when
they ask to be buried in her, or as a mother cowed by the blows of the
cruel sun-father" (9).

I resist the symbolic reading because, as with the treatment of the
seasons in *Waiting for the Barbarians*, there is something explicitly
conventional in the metaphor, as if, while allowing a certain scope to the
symbolism (and I shall return to this point), Coetzee were also offering
gardening as merely the convenient, structural opposite of power. The
structuralist notion that binaries are "machines" for the production of
discourse is a basic part of Coetzee's intellectual equipment. As Susan
Barton puts it—with some irony—in *Foe*: "it seems necessary only to

establish the poles, the here and the there, the now and the then—after that the words of themselves do the journeying. I had not guessed it was so easy to be an author" (93). If K lives in a "pocket outside time" (82), if he is "not in the war" (189), then "gardening" merely defines his preferred habitat, and his temporal universe becomes the seasonal cycle. As Coetzee says, K "can't hope to keep the garden because, finally, the whole surface of South Africa has been surveyed and mapped and disposed of. So, despite K's desires, the opposition that the garden provides to the camps is at most at a conceptual level" ("Two Interviews" 456).

Beyond its structural uses, however, the idea of gardening as cultivation does accumulate a certain *ethical* significance. Thinking of his first seeds, which he has to abandon just as they begin to sprout, K says: "There was a cord of tenderness that stretched from him to the patch of earth beside the dam and must be cut. It seemed to him that one could cut a cord like that only so many times before it would not grow again" (90). K's pumpkins and melons become his family, his brothers and sisters, suggesting, in attenuated form, the possibility of community. It will be recalled that *Barbarians* carries a similar muted theme in its representations of children. Michael K responds to the distress of the children in the Jakkalsdrif camp by forming a "protective circle" for one of them with his arms (124). Protectiveness, nurturing, cultivation: this thread involves an attempt, I suggest, to project a posthumanist, reconstructed ethics; certainly, the Magistrate's halting steps in this direction in *Barbarians* become elaborated more fully in *Michael K*. But the condition for such ethical reconstruction is a recognition of the pervasive intrusiveness of totalitarian violence.

LET THE BOOK GO TO WAR

The story of Michael K, as I have presented it, is told in parts 1 and 3 by an omniscient narrator in *style indirect libre*. The metafictional element is introduced in part 2, which presents the Medical Officer's first-person reflection on the meaning of K's story. The metaphor of parasitism finds another application here, for K becomes host to the Medical Officer, who figures as the hermeneutic parasite. However, Coetzee alerts his reader to the appropriating function of interpretation well before the Medical Officer begins his memoir. In Jakkalsdrif camp, in part 1, while observing the silence of a young mother whose child has died, K wonders whether the image of her stoicism is part of his "education," for the

scenes being enacted before him appear to cohere: "He had a presenti-
ment of a single meaning upon which they were converging or threaten-
ing to converge, though he did not know yet what that might be" (122).
Gradually, it becomes apparent to K that there is a relationship between
the way significances are distributed and the war itself; consequently, he
develops a set of reflexes that involve avoiding or circumventing stated
significances, even when they appear correct or to serve his own interests. For example, Robert acts as a "critical consciousness" in Jakkalsdrif,
making sound judgments that expose the corruption of those in authority and show the guilty side of charity in Prince Albert. K responds, "I
don't know . . . I don't know." Robert becomes angry: "You've been
asleep all your life. It's time to wake up" (121). Later, K imagines the
townspeople forcing the inmates to dig a hole deep enough to bury
themselves in so they might be properly forgotten, but then he adds: "It
seemed more like Robert than like him, as he knew himself, to think like
that" (130).

The idea of "knowing himself," however, is also problematic. This is
illustrated in what is perhaps the most politically sensitive point in the
novel, when K contemplates leaving the farm and his pumpkins to join
the rebels. Deciding not to go, he tells himself, "Enough men had gone
off to the war saying the time for gardening was when the war was over;
whereas there must be men to stay behind and keep gardening alive, or
at least the idea of gardening" (150). But K's rationale—which seems
plausible enough in the light of the metaphoric patterns previously
established—is immediately undermined: "Always, when he tried to
explain himself to himself, there remained a gap, a hole, a darkness
before which his understanding baulked, into which it was useless to
pour words. The words were eaten up, the gap remained. His was
always a story with a hole in it: a wrong story, always wrong" (150–51).

Before solid-seeming explanations, including this apparently crucial
one about his vocation and its role in the war, K typically feels anxious
and stupid. Even as a child such feelings would overwhelm him: in the
classroom at Huis Norenius he would sit staring at mathematical problems, waiting for words like *quotient* to unravel their mystery (150).
However, because K is never his own narrator, there is a sense in which
the narrator interpolates in this moment in such a way as to dramatize
narration's own limitations, that is, its own *willed* limitations. It is an
image of aporia, or stalled meaning. This image takes us into the
philosophical terrain of the Nietzschean "will to ignorance," standing as
the alternative to the devouring "will to truth," which, in this context, is

contiguous with the war. We are also entering the terrain, of course, of early Derridean deconstruction: K's meaning will never arrive, for his story is constituted in the play of identity and difference that defines textuality. We can therefore mention another implication in K's gardening at this point, namely the notion of *dissemination*: K's is "the seed that neither inseminates nor is recovered by the father, but is scattered abroad" (Spivak, "Translator's Preface" xi). There is a moment, to which I must now turn, when something closely resembling the Derridean concept of the *trace* is given a socially nuanced meaning.

In response to K's silence and refusal to be treated, the Medical Officer progresses from being K's nurturing protector to "persecutor, madman, bloodhound, policeman" (229). K's obduracy both fascinates and infuriates him: "He passes through these institutions and camps and hospitals and God knows what else like a stone. Through the intestines of the war" (185). Coetzee has described K as a figure of *being* rather than of *becoming* ("Two Interviews" 455); similarly, to the Medical Officer he is a "soul blessedly untouched by doctrine" (207). But the insertion of the Medical Officer's narration involves something other than Sartrean thematics (although this element is carried over, to some extent, from the first two novels), for it is the Medical Officer's *pursuit* of K that is finally at issue. The memoir turns into a letter addressed directly to K; then the Medical Officer imagines himself literally chasing K, desperately shouting his account and appealing for the wave of a hand in confirmation while K disappears into the thickets ahead. The Medical Officer himself has become an agent of the war. His interpretation of K is quite correct; indeed, it is the novel's most direct statement of what K represents: "Your stay in the camp was merely an allegory, if you know that word. It was an allegory—speaking at the highest level—of how scandalously, how outrageously a meaning can take up residence within a system without becoming a term in it" (228).

It is not the interpretation itself that ultimately matters, however; what is presented here is the capacity of the novel to "get behind" itself and displace the power of interpretation in such a way that K is left uncontained at the point of closure. This is how one might speak of K as the narratological figure of the Derridean trace. Coetzee's metafictional frame produces the deconstructive gesture of erasure. K's "essence" is allowed to slip back into the open-endedness of textuality from which it comes and to which it returns. Again, Gayatri Chakravorty Spivak provides the appropriate terminology for this move in her elucidation of Derrida's Nietzsche: "When the outlines of the 'subject' are loosened,

the concepts of figuration or metaphoricity—related to meaning-ful-
ness—are subsumed under the broader categories of appropriation and
the play of resistant forces" ("Translator's Preface" xxiv).

If the metafictional frame shifts the ground away from the nominal to
something else, to something like the grammatological, then in terms of
the logic of metafictionality itself, we are obliged to ask further questions about the implications of this shift, about the limits of a movement
that could, hypothetically, involve deconstruction's process of infinite
deferral. Coetzee himself instructs us to treat this question skeptically in
his own criticism when he inquires into Nabokov's reliance on the ironic
limitlessness of metafictional framing in *Pale Fire*. He argues that in
Nabokov there is a *defiant* (and, by implication, post-Romantic) attempt merely to *assert* the "primacy of art" over the power of history—
in this instance, "history-as-interpretation" ("Nabokov's *Pale Fire*"
1–7). As Coetzee points out, history is a metamyth that promptly
reappropriates such defiance by historicizing it. How do we interpret a
move on Coetzee's part that is similar to, though possibly less ingenuous
than, Nabokov's, accepting, in turn, that even as we ask this question
we, too, have entered a realm that Coetzee has refigured in the novel
literally as a battlefield?

Spivak's phrase "resistant forces" is apt. Something close to Gordimer's critical position on *Michael K* has been put to Coetzee directly.
Asked how he would reply to the charge of "furthering the liberal
fantasy of the politics of innocence and so obstructing progressive
action," Coetzee replied: "I have no wish to enter the lists as a defender
of Michael K. If war is the father of all things, let the objection you voice
go to war with the book, which has now had its say, and let us see who
wins" (Coetzee, "Two Interviews" 459). This war is a dangerous one for
writers and writing, though it grows out of the larger and, of course,
more cruel one. In a frenzied culture such as South Africa's (though, of
course, this turn has occurred elsewhere) every sign, no matter how
innocent, becomes a signifier at another level, pointing to the larger
conflict. Within such a context there is no such thing as an irreducible
element. This is the context that makes the phenomenon of K—to use
the Medical Officer's terminology—"scandalous" and "outrageous." K
is not a representative figure who models certain forms of behavior or
capacities for change; rather, he is an idea floated into a discursive
environment that is unprepared to receive it. The fact that questions
about the evasiveness of *Michael K* are put to Coetzee in interviews and
repeatedly raised in reviews and criticism merely confirms the conditions

that the novel itself enacts. The novel *anticipates* such probing, in fact, incorporating it into its own fabric in the image of its very obsessiveness. This tension informs *Life and Times of Michael K*, read as a document of South African culture.

The novel stages a conflict, then, over the symbolic value of narrating in order to sustain its own form of discourse in what it calls "the cauldron of history" (207). When we read the Medical Officer's realization—achieved through K's example—that he has been wasting his life "by living from day to day in a state of waiting," that he had "in effect given myself up as a prisoner to this war" (216), it is difficult to avoid the implication this realization has for the activity of fiction writing, particularly after the sense of directionlessness and indecision that pervades the conclusion to *Waiting for the Barbarians*. Projecting beyond the moment of the "end" involves not only a redefinition of the relations of power but also a relocation or repositioning of the authorial voice. It is not that social conviction is lacking in *Michael K*—its scenario of the future pays its respects to that requirement—but that the novel dramatizes the risks involved in finding a place from which to speak. This is its politics of agency. When Coetzee argues in his *Weekly Mail* Book Week address of 1987 for the right of fiction to establish its own rules as against the rules governing the production of historical discourse, he does so with the achievement of *Michael K* behind him, a fiction that works this principle into its own formal design. On the question of design, however, let me turn, by way of concluding these remarks on *Michael K*, to Coetzee's debt to Kafka.

THE KAFKA CONNECTION

The transfiguration of the elements of fiction to the field of writing is a developmental feature of Coetzee's novels, reinforced by the fictionalization of certain features of deconstruction, but it is in Kafka that this movement is clinched. There are obvious links between the state of civil anomie through which South Africa is passing in *Michael K* and the nightmarish world of *The Trial* and *The Castle*. Doubtless, "K" is a nod to these works; *The Castle* seems particularly relevant with its concern with the authority of the document, in the form of the letter, and the way texts and stories circulate.[4] However, the pertinence of Kafka is more specific: we find it focused in the stories, particularly "The Burrow."

In 1981, two years before the publication of *Michael K*, Coetzee published an essay in *Modern Language Notes* entitled "Time, Tense,

and Aspect in Kafka's 'The Burrow.'" It examines how Kafka attempts
to do away with the distance separating the time of the events narrated
(utterance) from the time of narration (enunciation); such a project,
Coetzee argues, is syntactically and logically impossible, but its impetus
comes from Kafka's concern with the notion of a breakdown in the
experience of time, where things continually collapse or threaten to
collapse into a timeless, iterative present. All Coetzee's novels share to
some extent Kafka's concern with the relation between narrative and the
experience of time. The essay ends, however, by contrasting "historical"
and "eschatological" conceptions of temporality. The eschatological is
an "everlasting present" in which narration itself, the voice of enunciation, resides:

> Now that the narrator has failed time and again to domesticate time using
> strategies of narrative (i.e., strategies belonging to historical time), his struc-
> tures of sequence, of cause and effect, collapsing each time at the "decisive
> moment" of rupture when the past fails to run smoothly into the present, that
> is, now that the construct of narrative time has collapsed, there is only the
> time of narration left, the shifting *now* within which his narrative takes place,
> leaving behind it a wake (a text) of failure, fantasy, sterile speculation: the
> ramifications of a burrow whose fatal precariousness is signalled by the
> whistling that comes from its point(s) of rupture. (579)

Kafka seems to offer to Coetzee a powerful image of a narrating subject
confronting its own limits of possibility, indeed, its own death. It is
fitting that Foucault, in his essay "Language to Infinity," should refer to
"The Burrow" when addressing the question of speaking to avoid death:
it is "quite likely," Foucault argues, "that the approach of death—its
sovereign gesture, its prominence within human memory—hollows out
in the present and in existence the void toward which and from which
we speak" (53). The reflexive moment in narrative, Foucault goes on to
say, is a kind of "wound," for the process of doubling back is really an
attempt on the part of writing to postpone death, to "conceal, that is,
betray the relationship that language establishes with death—with this
limit to which language addresses itself and against which it is poised"
(57). Coetzee's muted affirmation of textual freedom, his attempt to
produce the narratological equivalent of deconstruction's gesture of
erasure, gains force from this description because we are able to see it in
its sociocultural light. Kafka's creature in "The Burrow" is sustained by
a similar urgency: Gilles Deleuze and Félix Guattari's description of
Kafka as producing a "minor" literature, which involves writing in
German, in Prague, and as a Jew, clarifies the connection: Kafka's

narrative drive, in which "expression precedes content" (41), is a form of defense and resistance to entrapment.[5]

The closing lines of Michael K neatly illustrate these observations. Seeing himself returning to the farm, and finding the water pump blown up by the army, K imagines obtaining water:

> He, Michael K, would produce a teaspoon from his pocket, a teaspoon and a long roll of string. He would clear the rubble from the mouth of the shaft, he would bend the handle of the teaspoon in a loop and tie the string to it, he would lower it down the shaft deep into the earth, and when he brought it up there would be water in the bowl of the spoon; and in that way, he would say, one can live. (250)

Michael K presents us, finally, with an image of resistance in the open-endedness of writing, and it chooses as its field of operation not the transcendental framework of the making or unmaking of history but the social exchange of literature within a particular cultural context. The marginal freedom—what Foucault calls the "virtual space" ("Language to Infinity" 55)—of textuality, a freedom that can be celebrated only in proportion as it is seen to be historically constrained, is held up and circulated by the novel within a heavily politicized culture as a quality deserving more than casual acknowledgment.

FIGURES OF AUTHORITY

It is not surprising that Coetzee, having explored the social meaning of textuality, should subject the *authority* of textualization to such careful scrutiny in his next novel, Foe (1986). The later work represents a withdrawal from the achievement of Michael K to examine the historical and discursive conditions under which white South African authorship must operate—a typically cautious gesture of qualification on Coetzee's part. It might be said that this very skepticism, and the fictional forms that Coetzee finds to elaborate it in Foe, serve only to reinforce the freedom of textualization embodied in Michael K. There would be some truth in this observation; however, it seems more appropriate simply to ask whether Coetzee is able to balance the claim of freedom with an equally rigorous acknowledgment of constraint. I read Foe with this question in mind: How does Coetzee define the limits of whatever textual authority he is able to achieve?

Coetzee positions Foe in the discursive field of postcoloniality, but he does so in peculiarly South African terms. Based on a revision of

Robinson Crusoe, the novel develops a characterology of the relations of power between the metropolitan center and the settler-colonial and native sectors of colonial society. Returning from Bahia, where she has been searching for a lost daughter, Susan Barton is put off the ship after a mutiny; she is accompanied only by the dead body of the captain, whose mistress she had been. She swims ashore and finds herself on the island with Cruso and Friday. Friday has been mutilated: he has no tongue. Who did this, when or how it happened, we are never told. After their rescue by a passing merchantman, Cruso dies aboard ship and Susan and Friday are left to make their way in England.

After she arrives in England, Susan drafts a memoir, "The Female Castaway," and seeks out the author, Foe, to have her story told. Coetzee's novel comprises four parts: beginning with Susan's memoir, it continues in a series of letters addressed to Foe, letters that do not reach him because he is evading his creditors; it proceeds to an account of Susan's relationship with Foe and her struggle to retain control over her story and its meaning; and it ends with a sequence spoken by an unnamed narrator (possibly standing for Coetzee himself) who revises the history as we know it and dissolves the narration in an act of authorial renunciation. Throughout the novel, Friday's silent and enigmatic presence gains in power until it overwhelms the narrator at the end. As Ina Gräbe succinctly puts it, in paying more attention to the telling of the story than the story itself, the novel clearly participates in postmodernism's favoring of the signifier over the signified (147–48).

Although I support Gräbe's view, I also intend to show that in this case the signifier itself is localized in allusive ways in order to make this story of storytelling responsive to the conditions that writers like Coetzee are forced to confront. To appreciate the scope of Coetzee's allegory—and this novel seems more consistently allegorical than the preceding ones—we might invoke the legacy of Olive Schreiner. As Stephen Gray has shown in his classic description of the liberal-realist tradition, Schreiner's *Story of an African Farm* (1883) is written in a genre of antipastoralism that leaves to later writers a particularly focused account of the intransigence of the interior landscape, the stultifying effects of colonial culture, and the futility of attempts to live meaningfully in South Africa (Gray 150–54). Transcendence of these conditions is impossible, and death comes as a final defeat. Such is the fate of Lyndall, the novel's hero; in Waldo, Schreiner creates a figure of Emersonian wishfulness whose dying moments simultaneously confirm the prevailing conditions and surmount them in a rare moment of lyrical absorption into Nature. Schreiner's novel offers an interesting pairing partly because of the intriguing possibility that Michael K is Coetzee's Waldo: although Waldo perishes and K survives, they are both little men of the earth who do not fully inhabit their history. More important, though, I turn to Schreiner because in *Foe* Coetzee finds the means to fictionalize the watchful presence that can be seen—from a symptomatic perspective—standing behind such limited affirmations as there are in the tradition. Consider Schreiner, preparing for Waldo's ambiguous death:

> Waldo was at work in the wagon-house again. He was making a kitchen-table for Em. As the long curls gathered in heaps before his plane, he paused for an instant now and again to throw one down to a small naked nigger, who had crept from its mother, who stood churning in the sunshine, and had crawled into the wagon-house. From time to time the little animal lifted its fat hand as it expected a fresh shower of curls; till Doss, jealous of his master's noticing any other small creature but himself, would catch the curl in his mouth and roll the little Kaffir over in the sawdust, much to that small animal's contentment. . . . Waldo, as he worked, glanced down at them now and then, and smiled; but he never looked out across the plain. He was conscious without looking of that broad green earth; it made his work pleasant to him. Near the shadow at the gable the mother of the little nigger stood churning. Slowly she raised and let fall the stick in her hands, murmuring to herself a sleepy chant such as her people love; it sounded like the humming of far-off bees. (273)

By the end of the century, of course, Schreiner was to confront the question of race directly, notably in her indictment of colonial violence in *Trooper Peter Halket of Mashonaland*, but this moment in *African Farm* defines the structural limitations that white writers have had to deal with from Schreiner on. The mother's chant, blending into the circumambient lyricism of the landscape "like the humming of far-off bees," will, in Coetzee, become the silence of Friday, which "passes through the cabin, through the wreck; washing the cliffs and shores of the island, it runs northward and southward to the ends of the earth" (*Foe* 157).

Schreiner is taken to represent a turning away from a colonial literature of exploration and adventure to a critical acceptance of the South African locale (Gray 136). In the famous preface to the second edition, she herself enjoins her reader to see *African Farm* in this light: "Should one sit down to paint the scenes among which he has grown, he will find that the facts creep in upon him" (24). Although Magda, in *In the Heart of the Country,* has prepared the way in Coetzee's own oeuvre, Susan Barton's arrival on Cruso's island can be taken to represent Schreiner's moment: it implies the division of a previously monolithic colonizing subject and the emergence of a dialogic structure within what is now settler-colonial culture. Like Schreiner, Susan resists making an adventure out of the story of the island (*Foe* 67). Through Schreiner, moreover, this transition in South African literary history was gendered; indeed, one can argue that gender made it possible. Susan Barton's narrative replicates this feminist self-affirmation, specifically by taking the island conditions of *Robinson Crusoe* and overlaying them with the narrative of Defoe's *Roxana,* whose picaresque feminine hero's real name is, of course, Susan.

The image of a beleaguered, hopeful Susan Barton—in her struggle to get her story told and in her relationship with Foe, author and agent of authorization—is strongly reminiscent of Schreiner's situation in London in 1881–82, when she was looking for a publisher for *African Farm.* This resemblance is especially strong in Schreiner's account of walking in the rain in Regent Street, feeling that "everyone could know that what was stuck under my cloak was a rejected ms." (Rive 8). One of the paradoxes that Schreiner lived out was that, although she had made her break with the colonial adventure, it was nevertheless in the metropolis that she had to seek publication. Her situation with respect to the metropolis was one of both distance and proximity. Such is Susan Barton's lot, too: she protects her version of the island but needs Foe to authorize it, to provide access to tradition and the institution of letters.

For Susan, however, the relationship with Foe is such that the authority of literariness recedes infinitely before her, confirming her marginality and lack of completion; the novel's title therefore gives prominence to Susan's anxiety about having her reality, what she frequently calls her "substantiality," confirmed in narrative discourse. Foe is her watchful confessor, imaged more than once as a dark spider (48, 120). Teresa Dovey's thesis concerning the Lacanian associations of Coetzee's fiction seems to have a particular relevance here; but as Dovey has also shown, *Foe* dramatizes the Foucauldian notion of the "author-function" as a regulatory principle (*Novels of J. M. Coetzee* 333–34). Coetzee exploits the concept of the "fathering" of prose narrative through a parody of one of its "founders," Daniel Defoe. Annamaria Carusi has taken this process further in a materialist-psychoanalytic analysis of the novel as an allegory of narrative as a form of commodity in which a chain of association is created between notions of truth, the body, and story, to be installed and circulated as Law ("*Foe*" 137–39). The changes Coetzee makes to the original patronyms would seem to confirm the direction of these readings: Defoe's historical name was, of course, Foe before he gentrified it (Dottin 65); similarly, Coetzee reverts to "Cruso," the name of Defoe's long-standing friend Timothy Cruso, a dissenting minister who seems to have provided the name of Defoe's adventurer (T. Wright 243). In both instances Coetzee sheds a "preliterary" light on his protagonists in order to place the transformations of the "literary" in question.

Coetzee's Cruso is unmoved by Susan's desire for authorization. In fact, in his taciturn resistance and self-absorption, his refusal to keep a journal, his reluctance to do anything to save himself, he is quite unlike his model (being closer, if anything, to Defoe's model, Alexander Selkirk).[6] Susan reflects: "Cruso rescued will be a deep disappointment to the world; the idea of a Cruso on his island is a better thing than the true Cruso tight-lipped and sullen in an alien England" (35). Coetzee's differentiation of Defoe's narrative according to South African conditions really begins here, rather than with Susan, for Afrikaners began turning their backs on Europe at approximately the time Defoe was writing, entering the interior of the Western Cape as pastoralists in unequal competition with the Khoisan, against the wishes of the Dutch East India Company. The second narrative of *Dusklands* tells this story in terms of violence, but it is equally possible to tell it as a story of entrapment: not only is there a spatial entrapment for which an island in the Atlantic might serve as a suitable metaphor, but there is also a temporal and cultural entrapment in a time before the Enlightenment.

Coetzee brings these threads together in an image of seemingly futile labor: Cruso's terraces are enigmatic, but their principal function is that they provide *work* for Cruso and the enslaved Friday. Two cultural injunctions from the colonial past are invoked here. The first is Calvinism, which enjoins its adherents to labor on the road to perfection; an echo of Calvinism is found in Cruso's comment "I ask you to remember, not every man who bears the mark of the castaway is a castaway at heart" (33). The second injunction is linked to pastoralism, in which the land "is humanized when inscribed by hand and plough" (*White Writing* 7). This is a pastoralism of settlement rather than ownership. As Cruso says: "The planting is reserved for those who come after us and have the foresight to bring seed. I only clear the ground for them. Clearing ground and piling stones is little enough, but it is better than sitting in idleness" (33). Finally, Cruso's love of emptiness in the seascape and his irritation at being disturbed from his reverie (38) parallel

Coetzee's description in his Jerusalem Prize acceptance speech of the "failure of love" in South Africa, that is, the settler's love of the land and landscape at the expense of the polity ("Apartheid" 124).

Friday's differentiation within the South African situation is equally specific. As Coetzee himself has noted, in *Robinson Crusoe* "Friday is a handsome Carib youth with near-European features. In *Foe* he is an African" ("Two Interviews" 463). "The man squatted down beside me," says Susan, "He was black: a Negro with a head of fuzzy wool, naked save for a pair of rough drawers. I lifted myself and studied the flat face, the small dull eyes, the broad nose, the thick lips, the skin not black but dark grey, dry as if coated with dust" (5–6). Friday's contextualization is most clearly rendered, however, in his mutilation and lack of speech. This seems to be Coetzee's unique, and uniquely South African, contribution to the tradition of Robinsonades spawned by Defoe.[7] In his review of the novel Neville Alexander, a theorist of the national question and a linguist who spent many years on Robben Island, argues that the pertinence of Friday to black history is not in question: "The apparent inaccessibility of Friday's world to the Europeans in this story is an artist's devastating judgement of the crippling anti-humanist consequences of colonialism and racism on the self-confident white world" (38).

Collectively, therefore, Coetzee's protagonists represent the ambiguous condition of postcoloniality that South Africa inhabits. What distinguishes white South African literature from other "postcolonizing" literatures is not only that white South African literature is linguistically diverse but that the territorial capture underpinning it was always less complete; the consequence is a form of postcoloniality that, to the extent that it is critical, stands under an ethical and political injunction always to defer to the authority of an emergent nationalist resistance that will inaugurate the age of postcoloniality proper. When such a moment will arrive, and, indeed, whether such a moment will "arrive," what political form it might take, and whether there is a unitary voice that can be taken to model the nationalist alternative—these are all valid questions. Coetzee's approach to such issues, however, in the figure of Friday, is cautious: preferring not to presume too much, Coetzee allows the representation of Friday to be shaped by the obvious political and epistemological limitations of colonial discourse, a position from which even the critical, self-consciously marginal, and feminist colonial discourse represented by Susan cannot entirely escape. In other words, in Friday's silence Coetzee acknowledges where he stands while simultaneously fictionalizing the transformative power that threatens, or promises, to eclipse the voices of what we might call, for want of a better term, colonial postcolonialism.

Let me turn to *Foe* in more detail to demonstrate how its elements are set in motion. Susan's quest to get her story told begins as a desire for substantiality: "Return to me the substance I have lost, Mr Foe: that is my entreaty" (51). At this stage, her conception of Foe's power is that he can provide sufficient realistic detail to give her story the density of "truth." She tells herself that the word "story" means "a storing-place of memories" (59) and that language creates a "correspondence between things as they are and the pictures we have of them in our minds" (65). As she deepens herself in composing letters to Foe, however, she begins to find this version of truth to be unworkable. For one thing, her story lacks adventure, though she is also unwilling to invent episodes that did not happen. More seriously, she realizes that she does not know how to account for Friday's mutilation: "What we accept in life we cannot accept in history. To tell my story and be silent on Friday's tongue is no better than offering a book for sale with pages in it quietly left empty. Yet the only tongue that can tell Friday's secret is the tongue he has lost!" (67).

Later she reflects directly on the difficulties of writing stories, comparing it to Cruso's and Friday's labor on the terraces and speaking of it as requiring the power of divination, a power she lacks (87). She lists what she calls the "mysteries" of the island, a series of unresolved questions: What was the meaning of the terraces? How did Friday lose his tongue? Why did Friday submit to Cruso? Why did neither Cruso nor Friday desire her? What was the meaning of Friday's act of scattering petals on the water near the site where she imagines they were shipwrecked? Such questions remain unanswered. What we are witnessing in this sequence is Susan's increasing engrossment in language as resistant material; needless to say, even at this early stage of the process much of the intractability Susan feels can be ascribed to Friday's enigmatic presence.

But the appearance of a girl claiming to be Susan's daughter taxes her patience more than Friday at this point, and it is here that Coetzee introduces *Roxana*. Defoe's novel is the confessional narrative of a woman who achieves prosperity by living as a courtesan or, as she prefers to call herself, a "free woman"—a term that Susan Barton uses as well. Toward the end of the novel Defoe introduces the daughter, named Susan after her mother (whose identity as "Roxana" is thereby undermined), as a reminder of the children Roxana deserted when her first husband left her and she set off on her path to fortune and independence. Roxana refuses to acknowledge the daughter, who is subsequently murdered in a misguided act of service by the servant, Amy. She repudiates Amy but lives on in torment, the condition that generates the confession. With the return of the daughter, therefore, as John J. Richetti points out, "the center of the narrative shifts from the controlled external world of financial and sexual relationships, from clothes, rich furniture, investments and titles, to the controlling internal world of memory and guilt" (118). *Control* is the key here: Roxana's desire to remain author of her life is superseded by her past catching up with her, which turns her story into a morally ironic drama of psychological destiny. Her identity as the girl's mother is the essential ingredient in this transition: in a phrase suggestive of Coetzee's concerns, Roxana calls it "the grand reserved article of all" (*Roxana* 319).

In *Foe*, Susan Barton's desire to control her destiny is sustained in her repudiation of the daughter as Foe's own invention. Unlike *Roxana*, the embrace of the mother and daughter produces no memorable bonding. The daughter figures as the point of dispute between Susan and Foe in their different versions of Susan's narrative and of the role of the island in it: to Foe, once Susan returns to England, the daughter successfully takes up the quest abandoned by the mother, thus producing a neatly resolved plot; this resolution traduces Susan's account, which preserves the centrality of the island and leaves the daughter forever lost. Which of these versions is ultimately the "truth" is unimportant; what matters is that a struggle for control over the narrative is staged between Foe and Susan and that Susan does not succumb. In fact, it is possible to measure Susan's success in several ways. When she explains to the "daughter" that she actually has no mother, that she is "father-born" (91), she is responding to Foe's imposition, asserting her will at the same level as Foe's, that is, at the level of invention or plot construction. When she and Foe couple, she mounts him as the Muse, both "goddess and begetter" of her story (126). That she manages to effect a reversal of gender roles on Foe is clear when, not long thereafter, Foe imagines himself as Susan's "old whore" and Susan savors the thought of having turned Foe into her "mistress" and, finally, her "wife" (152). (This moment recalls the transvestism of *The Story of an African Farm*, when Gregory Rose dresses as a woman in order to attend to Lyndall on her deathbed [252–65]; perhaps gender reversal represents a pattern of

limited victory in the colonial feminist's desire for authorization in
South Africa.)

The question arises of whether Susan's assertions are enough to bring
her the substantiality she longs for; in this respect, her very determination gives the game away. On the journey to Bristol, during the fruitless
attempt to manumit Friday and return him to Africa, she discovers a
dead baby in a ditch and asks, "Who was the child but I, in another
life?" (105), as if at the core of her desire for self-representation she
senses a lack that will always leave her incomplete, inchoate. She nevertheless pursues her project to the point of despair: "Now all my life
grows to be story," she says to Foe, speaking of the daughter figure,
"and there is nothing of my own left to me. I thought I was myself and
this girl a creature from another order speaking words you made up for
her. But now I am full of doubt. I am doubt itself" (133).

Critics have responded to the uncertainties in Susan's quest in interesting ways, two of which I shall mention here. When Susan asserts a
counterstory to Foe's, she places the year on the island at the center. The
problem, however, is that Friday cannot be incorporated into this story:
his mutilation, his ritual of scattering petals on the water at the site
where Susan assumes he was shipwrecked, his subjectivity—all are
simply inaccessible to Susan. She says to Foe, "If the story seems stupid,
that is only because it so doggedly holds its silence. The shadow whose
lack you feel is there: it is the loss of Friday's tongue" (117). Dovey
discusses this inconsistency in terms of the intersection between feminist
and postcolonial discourses ("postcolonial" implying, in this case, anticolonial nationalism), arguing that Coetzee's purpose is to show how
the more prominent forms of Western feminism have appropriated the
colonized subject to their own ends, using the native Other as a convenient figure for feminine difference (*Novels of J. M. Coetzee* 356–66).
Spivak notices not only that the gendered position is strained but that
the novel strains to make it appear so; she then suggests, more positively,
that Coetzee wishes to demonstrate "the impossibility of restoring the
history of empire and recovering the lost text of mothering *in the same
register of language*" ("Theory in the Margin" 162–65). (It seems
possible, incidentally, to read Schreiner's life and career as partly an
attempt to reconcile these differences.)

To these arguments one must add that the feminism Coetzee constructs through Susan carries additional allegorical burdens that have
little to do with gender. In the allegory of white South African author-

ship, Susan's womanhood suggests the relative cultural power of the province as opposed to the metropolis and of unauthorized as opposed to authorized speech; gender therefore serves as the sign of the position of semimarginality that I have called colonial postcolonialism. In terms of the politics of agency, this is the position with which Coetzee identifies, and in an interview he has proved to be protective of this self-positioning. When asked whether *Foe*'s reflection on the book trade implied a critical retreat from the notion of being a "successful author," Coetzee responded with some asperity that the question was barbed, for it associated him with Foe whereas his sympathies in the novel were clearly with "Foe's foe, the *un*successful author—worse, author*ess*—Susan Barton" ("Two Interviews" 462). This comment can be taken as a measure of how gender is *complicated* through Susan, as the representative of a marginality that has more generalized implications.

FRIDAY, HISTORY, CLOSURE

Friday's inaccessibility, the "hole" in Susan's narrative (121), is the primary cause of her uncertainty, but this inaccessibility does not explain Friday's *power*. In the third and final sections of the novel Friday gains in stature as the site of a shimmering, indeterminate potency that has the power to overwhelm and cancel Susan's narrative and, finally, Coetzee's novel itself. How is this power achieved? The explanation seems related to the fact that Susan's story is partly confessional and that, as Coetzee argues in "Confession and Double Thoughts: Rousseau, Tolstoy, and Dostoevsky" (1984), the problem repeatedly thrown up by confession is the problem of closure. Friday possesses the key to the closure of the narrative. The economy of confession, Coetzee argues in the essay, is such that its self-examination is potentially endless; the self-directed skepticism of confession produces a questioning of the confessant's own motives, so that resolutions to confession that rely solely on the achievement of "truth" through the confessant's own self-scrutiny, without the intervention of grace that brings renunciation, can be taken only as disingenuous. The confessant does not have the power to end the discourse but merely to abandon it. The problem is illustrated in Foe's account of the woman in Newgate prison who kept confessing and throwing doubt on her confession until the chaplain simply pronounced her shriven, despite her protestations, and left her. Foe's moral is that "there comes a time when we must give reckoning of ourselves to the world, and then forever hold our peace," but Susan's deduction, which is nearer the mark, is that "he has the last word who disposes over the greatest force" (124). Susan's story is one of sheer will, of insistence, which is forever locked in a struggle with the Foe of its own authorization, a story of endless elaboration; its few little victories are temporary, for the struggle must continually reconstitute itself. It is not, therefore, a story with an end; furthermore, it is a story in which Friday will always remain the silent, subverting Other. Foe shrewdly suggests to Susan that "as it was a slaver's stratagem to rob Friday of his tongue, may it not be a slaver's stratagem to hold him in subjection while we cavil over words in a dispute we know to be endless?" (150).

There are important connections between Friday and closure, notably Friday's dancing and the question of castration. In *Roxana* the daughter remembers her mother's moment of triumph, dancing alone for the amusement of guests in what is passed off as a Turkish performance. Recalling the event, the daughter destroys the mother's carefully pre-served identity because it proves the *daughter's* identity and thereby Roxana's as well; thus, through the twist in the narrative the dance is first a means of securing Roxana's self-representation as Other, affirm-ing her sexuality and social ascendancy, and then, as it is recalled by the daughter, the means of her undoing. In *Foe* Friday dances in Foe's scarlet robe, whirling around so that Susan can satisfy her curiosity about whether, in his mutilation, he was also castrated. What Susan sees, however, we do not know:

> In the dance nothing was still and everything was still. The whirling robe was a scarlet bell settled upon Friday's shoulders and enclosing him; Friday was the dark pillar at its centre. What had been hidden from me was revealed. I saw; or, should I say, my eyes were open to what was present to them.
> I saw and believed I had seen, though afterwards I remembered Thomas, who also saw, but could not be brought to believe till he had put his hand in the wound. (119–20)

Defoe grants Roxana Otherness to construct her gendered difference and then takes it away in an act of unveiling; Coetzee does not allow Susan to assume this authority. Whatever the condition might be of Friday's body, the state of his potency, Susan is not able to tell us, for she does not dispose over this power. More strictly, neither Susan's dis-course nor the novel's can appropriate the image: "I do not know how these matters can be written of in a book," says Susan immediately afterwards, "unless they are covered up again in figures" (120). One might ask, what discourse could adequately represent Friday? The answer Susan and Foe give, of course, is *Friday's own discourse*: "We must make Friday's silence speak, as well as the silence surrounding Friday," says Foe (142). Only in this way will they see into the "eye" of the island, the eye lying below the surface of the water at the site of the imagined wreck, and the eye, indeed, that watches over Susan and Foe as the silent guardian of the story. Because Friday is mute, they try teaching him to write, beginning with words that would seem to evoke the data of his own history and experience: "house," "ship," "Africa." (This incident has the additional effect of questioning the self-confident practice of transcribing oral histories.)

When Friday makes his own marks on the slate, however, he produces "eyes, open eyes, each set upon a human foot; row upon row of eyes upon feet: walking eyes" (147). Friday's writing inscribes his own watchfulness over Susan and Foe: it produces tokens of his position as the "wholly Other" (Spivak, "Theory in the Margin" 157). The foot is Friday's trademark, of course; it is the footprint of *Robinson Crusoe* and every Robinsonade; in this case, however, the body of Friday *and* Friday's silent gaze are conjoined.

Shortly afterward, Friday installs himself at Foe's desk, assuming the position of authorship. As he sits poised with a quill, Susan intervenes: "He will foul your papers," she protests, to which Foe replies, "My papers are foul enough, he can make them no worse" (151). What Friday writes are "rows and rows of the letter *o* tightly packed together. A second page lay at his elbow, fully written over, and it was the same." "It is a beginning," says Foe; "Tomorrow you must teach him *a*" (152). Friday is writing *o*, omega, the sign of the end, whereas Foe desires that he produce the assimilable story of himself, starting at the beginning with *a*, alpha.[8] This scene follows Susan's acknowledgment that "we are all alive, we are all substantial, we are all in the same world," an observation that excluded Friday. In other words, Friday's power to close the discourse overrides even Susan's final, resigned acceptance that despite the incompleteness of her story, she shares with the daughter and with Foe a specific, historical materiality.

At this point we need to shift to the metafictional level. If Coetzee is able to dramatize Friday's power to override both Susan's desire for authorization and Foe's ability to grant it, is he not assuming control over such power, that is, appropriating it toward the goal of skeptical self-cancelling, of the self-representation of the consciously marginal writer? How does the ending of *Foe* deal with the possibility that the

novel itself might represent merely another attempt to make Friday
speak in the name of interests that are not his own?

Such a conclusion would be feasible were it not for *Foe*'s brief final
section, part 4, a metafictional excursus that takes this problem into
account. The question turns on *appropriation*, once again, as it did in
Michael K: Coetzee's problem is to find a suitable reflexive vehicle for
distancing himself from the appropriative gesture. The narrative structure thus far consists of four sections arranged in such a way that
gradually Susan speaks "in her own voice." Beginning with "The Female Castaway" (part 1), cited as a communication to Foe, the novel
becomes explicitly epistolary with Susan continuing to write to Foe
about her story (part 2); in part 3 there are no quotation marks because
Susan has taken up her own narrative, turning it into an account of the
relationship with Foe. In part 4 an unnamed narrator appears whose
addressee is not specified: in other words, we are now in the realm of
narration per se, and the addressee is simply the reader, the one who
holds the book. This moment represents the last phase of the gradual
process of "getting behind" the voice of narration that is staged from
beginning to end.

The unnamed narrator enters Foe's house twice, producing two
encounters with the scene of authorship. In the first sequence he passes
the daughter on the landing; Susan and Foe lie side by side in bed; all
three are dead. He finds Friday alive, feels a faint pulse, parts the teeth,
and listens: he hears "the faintest faraway roar," "like the roar of waves
in a seashell." "From his mouth, without a breath, issue the sounds of
the island" (154). The history that Susan was unable to tell is there; the
story of the island is still Friday's possession. Coetzee is careful, therefore, not to disqualify Friday from having a history, even though the
emphasis falls on the silence that Friday keeps within the context of
those authorized to speak. This does not mean, obviously, that the novel
can *represent* Friday's history; it simply means that Friday is acknowledged to have one.

In the second sequence the narrator sees a plaque on the wall declar-
ing unambiguously, "*Daniel Defoe, Author.*" We are now in the realm
of the literary history we knew before the appearance of *Foe*. What does
the narrator find? He finds the three protagonists, again dead, though
on this occasion Susan and Foe lie in a casual embrace—signifying,
perhaps, the de facto, unspoken collusion of the male tradition with its
unauthorized female counterpart, as seen from this, the colonial-

postcolonial perspective. The fact that Friday now has a scar on his neck, "like a necklace, left by a rope or chain" (155), unobserved before in the novel, would seem to confirm this reading. The narrator finds the dispatch box into which Susan has been depositing her writings, opens it, reads the documents, and enters the "The Female Castaway" where Susan had begun: "With a sigh, barely making a splash, I slip overboard" (155). This time, however, he goes straight to the "eye" of the story, the site of mysterious power in the sea over which Friday scattered his petals. (Susan spoke of storytelling as divination: here the narrator proposes to divine the source of Friday's power.) Pulling himself down underwater on trunks of seaweed, he locates the wreck and moves through it, finding on the way the remains of unfinished stories by Defoe, remains like the mud of Flanders, "in which generations of grenadiers now lie dead, trampled in the postures of sleep" (156). Eventually he finds Susan and, not Foe, but the ship's captain, "fat as pigs in their white nightclothes," floating against the roof (157). Susan's narrative and all that develops from it lie buried here: the story of Susan, Cruso, and Friday has never been written. The narrator continues searching and finds Friday, the symptomatic presence of all colonial narratives, seemingly dead but in fact not dead, outliving the stories that might or might not include him:

> I tug his woolly hair, finger the chain about his throat. "Friday," I say, I try to say, kneeling over him, sinking hands and knees into the ooze, "what is this ship?"
> But this is not a place for words. Each syllable, as it comes out, is caught and filled with water and diffused. This is a place where bodies are their own signs. It is the home of Friday. (157)

Friday's home is the body: his existence is a facticity that simply asserts its own priorities. The trials of marginal authorship are irrelevant to Friday. This ending amounts to a deferral of authority to the body of history, to the political world in which the voice of the body politic of the future resides. The final image is an act of renunciation before the overwhelming authority, the *force*, of the body politic now emergent in history:

> His mouth opens. From inside him comes a slow stream, without breath, without interruption. It flows up through his body and out upon me; it passes through the cabin, through the wreck; washing the cliffs and shores of the island, it runs northward and southward to the ends of the earth. Soft and

cold, dark and unending, it beats against my eyelids, against the skin of my face. (157)

To be true to its purposes, and to its carefully positioned political deference, *Foe* cannot *name* this force as "nationalism," as "anticolonial" rather than "colonial" postcolonialism, or provide any such formulation; strictly speaking, the novel must end with an act that Annamaria Carusi correctly calls "neutralization." Carusi explains: "Where a body has no possibility of splitting off into a representation ... where there is no possibility ... of grasping it within a subject-object relation, and therefore of signifying it by means of a signifying and signified unit ... that body is totally outside of our intelligibility: it is for us, nothing other than the void of death" (*"Foe"* 142). *Foe* ends, in other words, with an image in which the absolute limits of its own powers of authorization and signification are defined.

FIVE

Conclusion

Age of Iron

Coetzee's most recent novel represents both summation and departure. It remains for me to outline, therefore, the long-term transitions found in the first five novels, to locate these in *Age of Iron* (1990), and, finally, to suggest how this novel extends and enriches Coetzee's whole novelistic corpus. As it is with conclusions, my argument will be brief and schematic; I have no doubt that Coetzee will continue to produce pathbreaking fiction and that future novels will necessitate qualifications and revisions that I cannot anticipate.

The corpus of Coetzee's work from *Dusklands* to *Foe* undergoes three seismic shifts. The first shift involves the problem of authority. From a combative, aggressive subversion of the authority of colonialism and its discourses, Coetzee's fiction develops toward a point of self-conscious deference, marginality, even abnegation. Friday's silence is the culmination of this development, for here Coetzee takes his reader as far as it is logically possible to go into a recognition and dramatization of the historical constraints that influence his fiction writing. Having challenged the authority of the colonial legacy and the forms of ideology that obscured its destructiveness, Coetzee begins interrogating the discursive authority in whose name the subversion is enacted. Collectively, the novels illustrate Coetzee's contention, in the conclusion to his essay on the farm novel and *plaasroman*, that although "our ears today are finely attuned to modes of silence," it is a form of reading that, "subverting the dominant, is in peril, like all triumphant subversion, of becoming the dominant in turn" (*White Writing* 81). Coetzee's fiction declines such triumphalism, providing in its place a clear-eyed representation of its own historical positioning and the limits of its power.

In the second shift Coetzee moves away from an emphasis on discourse as an ideological structure in which the subject is pinioned, doomed to live out the forms of subjectivity imposed by history; rather, in the later fiction textuality emerges as a self-generating, protean dynamic that opposes the fixed structures of historical consciousness. This transition parallels developments taking place in his linguistic and literary critical scholarship: throughout the 1970s, in his work in stylistics Coetzee was drawn to the possibility that epistemologies could be located in the structures of language; by the mid-1980s—especially in the essay on confession in Rousseau, Tolstoy, and Dostoevsky, which is Coetzee's most substantial single piece of criticism—he is emphasizing the limitlessness of textuality or, more strictly, the relationships between limitlessness, self-knowledge, and forms of closure. In *Foe* we find a mode of textuality that, although conscious that it can be forced into silence, involves an endlessly elaborating skepticism that makes it virtually impossible to impose on it a symptomatic diagnosis of its "unconscious." Indeed, Coetzee's form of self-conscious textuality continually reaches into itself and uncovers the conditions of its own production—until a final limit appears that is simply the impossibility of further elaboration, the limit of silence or death.

In the third shift Coetzee rejects liberal humanism as an ideology useful to the colonial enterprise and begins to propose the necessity, certainly the desirability, of a reconstructed ethics in which certain traditional liberal values find a new relevance within an all-consuming and humanly damaging political struggle. *Dusklands* revels at times in aggressiveness, and its exposure of colonial violence is a deliberate affront to the evasions of liberal humanism; in *Waiting for the Barbarians* and *Life and Times of Michael K*, however, Coetzee begins to suggest that there is some distance between, on the one hand, recognizing or refusing the compromises of liberal humanism and its unwillingness to confront the inherent violence of colonialism and, on the other hand, abandoning altogether its traditional respect for the quality of human relationships and the social body in which they are formed. The need for reciprocity, the integrity of childhood, the possibility of community, the status of compassion or charity—such values surface more and more frequently in Coetzee's writing as haunting reminders of a kind of historical deprivation suffered by the people as a whole. The deprivation takes root, it must be said, with the arrival of the settler. As the epigraph to *White Writing* puts it, in lines drawn from Ovid's *Metamorphosis*: "Pressing his lips to foreign soil, greeting the unfamiliar mountains and plains, Cadmus gave thanks. . . . Descending from above, Pallas told him to plow and sow the earth with the serpent's teeth, which would grow into a future nation." Coetzee's ethicalism is stripped of liberal ideology and infused with historical sensitivity.

If *Foe* presents a questioning of narrative authority, *Age of Iron* puts a harder case: What does it mean to write *without* authority? Elizabeth Curren is dying of cancer in a society wracked with another kind of malignancy, a society given over entirely to the contest for power. This is not a contest for ideological hegemony; the struggle over ideas has ceased, and now either the state or the people will prevail. The police have a free hand under emergency regulations to dispense casual injury or death at random, and they do so; on the other side, the young militants of the townships have resorted to a hardened rhetoric of absolutes, sacrificing their youth to the all-encompassing demands of the struggle. Coetzee is responding to conditions during the worst years of the States of Emergency, 1986–1989—also the years given for the novel's composition. Perhaps the most striking feature of this period, politically, was the warfare conducted by the security forces against the insurrectionary youth, who were inspired in turn by a notion of "ungovernability" defined by the exiled political leadership, partly in response to the growing mood of the townships and the internal successes of the United Democratic Front. Coetzee uses two memorable slogans of the period: "liberation before education" (62) and "freedom or death" (149). Although several of the novels are similarly referenced to particular moments in contemporary South African history, Coetzee seems far less chary in *Age of Iron* about using representational discourse. The wet squalor of Cape Town's squatter camps, the cruelty of black vigilantes, the brutal efficiency with which the police kill comrades accused of belonging to underground cells—Coetzee incorporates such features of the conflict directly into his portrayal. "Friday," too, speaks in this novel, in the full authority of his appropriation of power. Indeed, the black voices in *Age of Iron* are articulate and diverse, from the simple, uncompromising declarations of Bheki and his activist friend, to the self-assurance of Florence, Elizabeth's char, and, finally, to the chilly eloquence of Thabane, the teacher turned tradesman who puts the comrades' case to Elizabeth with steely accuracy.

Characteristically, however, *Age of Iron* also goes much further than the representation of political conditions. The Other in *Age of Iron* is no longer the historical Other of colonialism: with black speech fully "represented," the interlocutor changes as well, becoming the taciturn derelict Vercueil, Elizabeth's consort and Angel of Death. The silencing of discourse is therefore no longer simply a function of political power, as it is in *Foe*; it has now become associated with the event of death itself. Three familial deaths are mentioned in the novel's dedication; the shift beyond the historical Other would seem to be connected to personal bereavement. But whatever its origin, Coetzee's question is this: What kind of discourse emerges from a narrative subject who has not made peace, exactly, with the historical Other, but for whom there is *another kind of limit* against which to speak? From the point of view of the subject, after all, the "final horizon" cannot be the broadly historical—as we have become accustomed to saying—but if so, is it not possible for the novel to stage a "conflict of limits"? What kind of discourse would such a conflict produce? These are the terms on which *Age of Iron* is built. Let me return, at this point, to the three categories raised earlier in the discussion of Coetzee's development, namely those of authority, textuality, and ethics.

While "the country smoulders," Elizabeth says, her attention "is all inward, upon the thing, the word, the word for the thing inching through my body. An ignominious occupation, and in times like these ridiculous too, as a banker with his clothes on fire is a joke while a burning beggar is not" (36). If Elizabeth has any authority, it is provided by her very irrelevance; it is the authority of the disparaged, of a retired lecturer in classics whose canon means little to anyone but herself, undergoing a private death.

On textuality, Elizabeth says, "Death may indeed be the last great foe of writing, but writing is also the foe of death. Therefore, writing, holding death at arm's length, let me tell you that I meant to go through with it, began to go through with it, did not go through with it" (106). Elizabeth is speaking here of her ridiculous plan to immolate herself in front of the Houses of Parliament, partly as a condemnation of the crimes of the state but also as a way of making her private death a public one, thus altering the scale on which it is valued. This does not happen; her death remains private. Her writing takes the form of a letter addressed to a daughter who has emigrated to America and will have nothing more to do with South Africa, at least not until the present rulers have passed on. The letter becomes a "rope of words" (181) that binds the daughter to the mother, forcing her to hear Elizabeth out. What Elizabeth says is no more important, in this configuration, than the fact that she finds a way to speak: *writing* becomes Elizabeth's mode of temporary self-preservation.

The skepticism and inconsequentiality of Elizabeth's discourse enable her to say exactly what she pleases about the way the national conflict is conducted. The ethicalism of *Age of Iron* emerges from this paradox. Elizabeth's judgment of the rule of white nationalism, the rule of the "boars," is direct and unsubtle. On the insurrection she is harsh, indeed confessional, in her condemnation of the new forms of puritanism and militarism evident in the township youth. To Thabane, for example, she says:

> I fear I know comradeship all too well. The Germans had comradeship, and the Japanese, and the Spartans. Shaka's impis too, I'm sure. Comradeship is nothing but a mystique of death, of killing and dying, masquerading as what you call a bond (a bond of what? Love? I doubt it). I have no sympathy with this comradeship. You are wrong, you and Florence and everyone else, to be taken in by it and, worse, to encourage it in children. It is just another of those icy, exclusive, death-driven male constructions. That is my opinion. (137)

These opinions count for nothing: she and Thabane "agree to differ." Thus, *Age of Iron* takes the process of ethical reconstruction further, but it does so by disclaiming the authority of the narrator. We need to ask, What kind of authority is it that rests on the assertion of its own irrelevance? Or more specifically: What conditions in South Africa, pertaining to ethical judgment, produce such a circuitous mode of address? The answer lies in the fact that ethical consciousness in South Africa is constrained because judgment is invariably selective or interested. The Magistrate's attempts in *Waiting for the Barbarians* to appeal to simple standards of decency were crippled by their complicity. Complicity is the result of having a constituency, of speaking (wittingly or not) on behalf of a group of dominant actors in the conflict. Within such conditions, speaking *without* authorization, or with an authority few are willing to take seriously in a society in which the "line" is a carefully managed mechanism for conducting the war rhetorically, could be one way in which ethical judgment can be partially restored.

The novel dramatizes this tension precisely: asked to "name the crime" she has witnessed on seeing a party of vigilantes burning the shacks of families suspected of sympathizing with the comrades, Eliza-

beth says such sights are to be condemned, but she "cannot denounce
them in other people's words. I must find my own words, from myself.
Otherwise it is not the truth" (91). Such expressions of misgiving or
restraint about how judgment is exercised could be said to constitute an
attempt on Coetzee's part to restore judgment to the public sphere—or,
at least, to imagine judgment being restored there. Speaking of
Gordimer's treatment of cruelty in *Burger's Daughter*, Coetzee said in
1986—the year he began working on *Age of Iron*—that what Rosa
Burger anticipates is "a time when humanity will be restored across the
face of society," a time "when all human acts . . . will be returned to the
ambit of moral judgement. In such a society it will once again be
meaningful for the gaze of the author, the gaze of authority and author-
itative judgement, to be turned upon scenes of torture" ("Into the Dark
Chamber" 35).

Coetzee's skepticism, his deferential handling of the politics of
agency, have prevented him, thus far, from projecting forward to a
moment such as this. Although *Waiting for the Barbarians* explores two
versions of temporality defined by Frank Kermode, namely *kairos* and
chronos, it omits Kermode's third term, which is *pleroma*, the "fullness
of time." Coetzee's *pleroma*, it seems, would be the restoration of
judgment, or at least the creation of conditions in which judgment
would become possible once again. Such a moment is projected nega-
tively in *Age of Iron* in the dramatization of the *failure* of reciprocal
judgment before scenes of cruelty:

> "This woman talks shit," said a man in the crowd. He looked around.
> "Shit," he said. No one contradicted him. Already some were drifting away.
> "Yes," I said, speaking directly to him—"you are right, what you say is
> true."
> He gave me a look as if I were mad.
> "But what do you expect?" I went on. "To speak of this"—I waved a
> hand over the bush, the smoke, the filth littering the path—"you would need
> the tongue of a god."
> "Shit," he said again, challenging me. (91)

In summary, *Age of Iron* shows that the transitions taking place in
Coetzee's novels are inexplicable except as the consequence of a consistent and increasingly refined sense of the historicity of fictional discourse
under South African conditions. This is true of the forms of authority
the novels invoke and scrutinize, the notions of textuality they inscribe,
and the ethical consciousness they propose or prepare for.

Age of Iron provides a lucid image of this complex historicity that emerges from a developmental reading of Coetzee's writing. Examining a photograph of her two American grandsons paddling a canoe in a recreational resort, Elizabeth cruelly tells her daughter that "it dispirits me that your children will never drown. All those lakes, all that water: a land of lakes and rivers; yet if by some mischance they ever tip out of their canoe, they will bob safely in the water, supported by their bright orange wings, till a motor-boat comes to pick them up and bear them off and all is well again" (178). She then adds:

> By no means do I wish death upon them. The two boys whose lives have brushed mine are in any event already dead. No, I wish your children life. But the wings you have tied on them will not guarantee them life. Life is dust between the toes. Life is dust between the teeth. Life is biting the dust.
>
> Or: life is drowning. Falling through water, to the floor. (179)

In a novel which is so much about dying, it is ironic that one of Elizabeth's responses to her daughter—whose own form of "iron" is her unbending will never to return—is to declare that *she* is the one passing on a legacy of death. In an interview with the *Washington Post*, Coetzee glosses this moment as follows:

> There is a certain controversy, isn't there, going on right at the moment in the United States about the "end of history"? . . . The position, expressed in a very crude way, is that the Western democracies have reached a stage in historical development in which development ceases because there is no stage beyond it. For better or worse liberal democracy is the form toward which all history tends. . . . That very way of seeing the history of mankind is a symptom of the First World . . . moving to a plateau of inconsequentiality or irrelevance. It's actually the Third World where history, real history, is happening. And the First World has played itself out of the game. (Coetzee, "Author on History's Cutting Edge," C4)[1]

The passage, and this statement, must bring us to the end of our study, for they return us to the site of history and present it, remarkably in Coetzee, as a place of privilege. Between the publication of the novel and this gloss, of course, lies a crucial moment in South Africa's history, namely February 1990, which saw the unbanning of exiled organizations, the release of numbers of political prisoners, and tentative negotiations toward a transition to democracy. This shift partly explains Coetzee's relative optimism. A year later, negotiations proper had not yet begun and the country was still riven with violence; at that point, Coetzee might have been less sanguine. But the statement is less a reflection of the current state of affairs in South Africa than a reminder of the extent to which historicity has informed Coetzee's oeuvre from the very beginning. In hindsight we can see that Coetzee's return to South Africa at the start of the 1970s had the effect of ensuring that his fiction would escape the consequences of the "posthistorical" age, that ultimately we would find in his novels a dramatic confluence of postmodern ideas and the history-making exigencies of a society in turmoil.

There can be no such thing, of course, as living "outside" history. Coetzee's novels have been rigorous in developing a sense of the situatedness of their subjects. But these novels have also projected themselves *beyond* their situation, alerting us to the as yet unrealized promise of freedom. Let me conclude by returning to the epigraph at the beginning of this study, to Coetzee's remark that he sees his novels as representations of "people slipping their chains and turning their faces to the light." In its encounter with the brutality of South Africa, and having absorbed the epistemological insecurities of postmodernism, Coetzee's fiction is more than conscious of its own precariousness. It is as vulnerable, in fact, as Elizabeth Curren's long letter to her daughter, entrusted to the hands of the drunken Vercueil after her death. Yet in *Age of Iron*, which is Elizabeth's text, South Africa means not only death—the renunciation of authority and the end of discourse—but also, because it is these things, the "dust between the teeth," an engagement with history that is in itself an act of transcendence.

Notes

NOTES TO INTRODUCTION

1. In South Africa, Coetzee has won the Mofolo-Plomer prize, the CNA prize (three times), the University of Cape Town Book Award, and the Pringle Prize for Criticism (twice). Internationally, he has won the Geoffrey Faber and James Tait Black Memorial prizes, the Booker-McConnell Prize, the Prix Femina Étranger, the Jerusalem Prize, and the *Sunday Express* Book of the Year Award. He is an honorary member of the Modern Languages Association and a Fellow of the Royal Society of Literature; he also holds honorary degrees from the University of Strathclyde and the State University of New York at Buffalo.

2. The most pertinent essays are Michael Vaughan, "Literature and Politics"; Paul Rich, "Apartheid"; Peter Knox-Shaw, "*Dusklands*"; and Peter Kohler, "Freeburghers."

3. Since Teresa Dovey's work, another book-length study has appeared, Dick Penner's *Countries of the Mind*. From a South African point of view, Penner's ethical universalism places him firmly in the metropolitan context; Penner's title is, among other things, a candid acknowledgment and defense of his critical detachment from South Africa (see "Preface" xv). Dovey's introduction to *J. M. Coetzee: A Bibliography* (Goddard and Read) provides a preliminary survey of the various contexts of reception of Coetzee's fiction, a question that merits further attention.

4. I have written more extensively on Dovey's *Novels of J. M. Coetzee* in "The Problem of History in the Fiction of J. M. Coetzee."

5. One of the more direct of political indictments comes from Michael Chapman, who, in a review of Dovey's *Novels of J. M. Coetzee*, dismisses *Foe* as providing "a kind of masturbatory release, in this country, for the Europeanising dreams of an intellectual coterie" (335). See *Journal of Literary Studies* 5.2 (1989), which represents the proceedings of a two-day seminar on *Foe* held at the

University of South Africa in March 1988, at which this conflict repeatedly surfaced. Annamaria Carusi studies this situation closely in "Post, Post, and Post."

6. Because some of my inferences from the nonfiction are put to Coetzee directly in J. M. Coetzee, *Doubling the Point*, the proper place for interested readers to look for intellectual biography is in those dialogues.

NOTES TO CHAPTER ONE

1. Although Coetzee does not follow Beckett down this path of eventual self-cancellation, parody and binary patterning do appear later in Coetzee's own stylistic repertoire as evidence of Beckett's lasting influence.

2. Coetzee might also have been drawn to the mathematical dimensions of Beckett's prose because of his own background in mathematics and computer programming; his early publications include essays in stylostatistics and experiments in computer-generated poetry and stylistic analysis.

3. "Much of my academic training was in Linguistics. And in many ways I am more interested in the linguistic than in the literary side of my academic profession. I think there is evidence of an interest in problems of language throughout my novels. I don't see any disruption between my professional interest in language and my activities as a writer" (Coetzee, "Interview de J. M. Coetzee" 43–44).

4. This debate has received new impetus both from Ndebele's ongoing theoretical clarification of what he calls "progressive formalism" and from Albie Sachs's controversial in-house seminar with the ANC, which proposes that talk of culture as a "weapon of struggle" in South Africa be banned for a period of five years in the interests of imaginative diversity and tolerance (Ndebele, "Actors and Interpreters"; Sachs, "Preparing Ourselves for Freedom.")

5. After the events of 1990, the weaknesses of such positions stand out more clearly: there is an ambiguity about the ethnic and class character of the oppressed groups being referred to, since the position of nationalist mass struggle, although politically ascendant, cannot but be unspecific about the meaning of the collectivity being mobilized; the stress on realism runs into the problem raised by Nkosi and Ndebele, the problem of epistemological transformation; the insistence on a formal alliance raises for many artists the specter of an internal, Stalinist policing. These questions and others are debated in the many responses to Albie Sachs's seminar (see note 4), collected in de Kok and Press, *Spring Is Rebellious*.

6. It is not only in cultural production that South Africans find themselves polarized in this way. In the social sciences, adherents of an E. P. Thompsonian movement that produces underclass and "people's" microhistories stand off against political sociologists, the local heirs of Louis Althusser and Nicos Poulantzas, in an acrimonious debate about the nature of resistance and the structural relationships between capitalism and apartheid. For example, see Morris, "Social History."

7. See Jan Haluska, "Master and Slave." Haluska takes Scholes's definition as his point of departure. The most common terms for the description of self-conscious narrative are *reflexivity, metafiction, fabulation, parody,* and *allegory.* My general description of Coetzee's novels as situational metafiction is not intended to be exclusive; I use other terms as the particular strategies of the novels demand.

8. The term *situational metafiction* might be compared with Linda Hutcheon's recent delineation of what she calls "historiographic metafiction" (*Poetics of Postmodernism* 105–23). Much of Hutcheon's analysis of postmodernism's renegotiation of the relations between fiction and history is applicable to Coetzee, and, indeed, she refers at some length to *Foe* (107–8). I retain the "situational" emphasis, however, which emerges from the total context in which the formal theorizing is done in this chapter.

9. In this discussion of agency I am indebted to Tony Morphet, "Brushing History Against the Grain."

10. See, for instance, Nicholas Visser, "Beyond the Interregnum."

11. Further historical descriptions are given at the beginnings of chapters 3 and 4. *Waiting for the Barbarians* and *Life and Times of Michael K* refer obliquely to particular aspects of the state's response to this crisis.

12. I am grateful to Andrew Nash for sharing with me his insights on the 1970s in South Africa and for drawing my attention to the Schlebusch Commission.

NOTES TO CHAPTER TWO

1. In *A Theory of Parody* Linda Hutcheon discusses the ambivalence in parody between "conservative repetition and revolutionary difference" (77). The conservative element involves parody's implied respect for tradition, which must complicate the popular view that parody and satire are interchangeable, for parody is not necessarily critical. Considered in these terms, Coetzee's use of parody is complex and changing. *Dusklands*'s parody of colonial discourses is bleak, at times aggressive; in the later fiction, however, the parodied texts, such as *Robinson Crusoe* and *Roxana,* apart from being more literary, are treated with more respect.

2. The extent to which Coetzee was grappling with the critical implications of fiction's address to readers can be gauged by his article "The First Sentence of Yvonne Burgess's *The Strike*" (1976), which appeared between the publication of the first two novels. Reading the codes of the Novel from the first line of Burgess's work, Coetzee argues that the book reaffirms a "social and character-ological typology" that ultimately assists in the consolidation of a "class bond" (48) in the circulation of literature. Coetzee's decision to decline the position of omniscience in the early novels is in opposition to this effect.

3. For example, Michael Vaughan describes this structure as defining a mode of consciousness that he calls "Northern European Protestant," which is said to be "identical" in both contexts (123); similarly, Peter Knox-Shaw argues that the

two-part structure involves the attempt to "universalise from the particular" (35).

4. The Jacobus Coetzee of the second part of *Dusklands* is based on an actual ancestor (see the commentary later in this chapter on Coetzee's parody of archival documents). However, in keeping with J. M. Coetzee's efforts to complicate historical knowledge in the moment of narration, he also names Eugene Dawn's supervisor "Coetzee." The effect is a retreat from conventions that preserve notions of authorial authenticity and objectivity.

5. "Eugene," which also means "noble" or "well-born," could be a reference to Eugene McCarthy. An actual "New Life Hamlet" project was undertaken in the context of "RD" (Revolutionary Development or Rural Development) strategies in Vietnam (a substrategy of what was called "pacification"). The "New Life Hamlet" project involved an attempt to recreate the traditional hamlet in order to encourage resistance to the infiltration of the Viet Cong in South Vietnam (Armbruster et al. 377–85). In *The Backroom Boys* Noam Chomsky records a number of similar, though jauntier, titles for operations: Phoenix, Rolling Thunder, Speedy Express, and Sunrise. In "The New Life Project," therefore, Coetzee allows history to provide the terms of its own allegorical diagnosis.

6. I am grateful to David Bunn for the term *ontological shock*.

7. In "Representing the Colonized" Edward Said notes the explicitly congruent interests of traditional anthropology and the U.S. Department of Defense. Similarly, Coetzee mentions Franz Boas as part of the mythographer's heritage.

8. Coetzee uses the term *mythographic* in reference to white nationalist history in "Man's Fate in the Novels of Alex La Guma," published in the same year as *Dusklands*.

9. This essay was subsequently reproduced in N. A. Coetzee's compendious (six-hundred-page) volume of Coetzee genealogy, *Die Stamouers Coetzee en Nageslagte*, published to commemorate the Coetzee family's three hundred years in South Africa. I am grateful to Catherine Glenn-Lauga for showing me this volume and for alerting me to *Bouvard et Pécuchet*.

10. In these descriptions of frontier terror, J. M. Coetzee is simply describing what was, indeed, a policy of genocide. I have not found any descriptions of procedure, as it were, of which Coetzee's version might be a parodic copy, but in Moodie's *Record* there are any number of reports of raids on camps, with numbers shot (usually men) or captured (usually women and children). In his journal of 1809 Colonel Collins reports meeting with one commando leader who could account for 3,200 dead, and another for 2,700 (Moodie, part 5 [1808–19], p. 7). Coetzee's version, it must be said, refuses the palliative of third-person objectification offered by statistics such as these; instead, he provides us with the implicated subject (see note 2).

11. Magda's condition would also exemplify what Jameson (following Lacan) calls "schizophrenia," the breakdown of the signifying chain, with the effect that a unified personal identity, connecting past, present, and future, cannot be constructed from broken units of discourse ("Postmodernism" 72).

12. Josephine Dodd explores themes of entrapment and escape with particular reference to gender in her discussion of *In the Heart of the Country*.

13. The schoolmistress, a "daughter of an impoverished clergyman, sent out to earn a living," who "ran away with a passing Englishman and was never heard of again" (45–46), would seem to be an allusion to both Schreiner and her fictional hero Lyndall in *The Story of an African Farm*. Teresa Dovey explores a range of further intertextual connections between the two novels in the second chapter of *The Novels of J. M. Coetzee*.

NOTES TO CHAPTER THREE

1. See Michael Vaughan: "In terms of formal organization, [*Barbarians*] has much less to discomfort the liberal reader than the earlier novels. The protagonist, too, appears to be much closer to the protagonists of liberal fiction, although he is certainly not identical to them. Is Coetzee moving towards a greater sympathy with liberal perspectives?" (125–26). Richard Martin argues a similar case at greater length. I believe Martin is in error, and for the most part I leave it to the reader to decide on the extent to which my reading provides an adequate reply. However, two mistakes in Martin's reading need to be addressed. First, he harnesses Robbe-Grillet in support of the argument that *Barbarians* is "a sort of existential tragedy in which the significance of objects and events is their lack of significance" (15). This use of Robbe-Grillet against Coetzee ignores Coetzee's own assimilation of the *nouveau roman* and his deployment of some of its conventions in the previous novel, *Heart of the Country*. The development from the earlier novel to this one involves, broadly speaking, a shift of emphasis from the ontological to the discursive. Second, it must be said that treating Coetzee as uncritical of naturalized language and Gordimer as an archproponent of narrative experimentation is an eccentric position, considering how these writers are usually contrasted. (I make the observation while recognizing that a sharp polarization can also be misleading.)

2. In "The Presence of Absence" Lance Olsen gives a Derridean reading of *Barbarians*, arguing that it "places civilization, authority, humanism and truth under erasure by disclosing the zero that beats at their centres" (47). I agree to an extent with Olsen's reading, but like both Barbara Eckstein and Susan Van Zanten Gallagher, who also begin by agreeing with Olsen, I do not believe that this "disclosure" necessarily diminishes the historical and ethical power of the work. In Olsen's hands a deconstructive reading removes the novel from notions of "responsibility"; by contrast, Eckstein and Gallagher, though working independently and with different theoretical and political premises, have written analyses of *Barbarians* that illuminate the relations between language, the body, torture and the state.

3. "The Agentless Sentence as Rhetorical Device" (1980), "The Rhetoric of the Passive in English" (1980), and "Newton and the Ideal of a Transparent Scientific Language" (1982).

4. See also Peter Skalnik, "Tribe as Colonial Category," especially p. 70. Jean-Phillipe Wade points out that similar forms of binarism (Europe-Africa, black-white, colonizer-colonized, settler-indigenous) were evident in the language of the Black Consciousness movement, which dominated resistance organizations in the late 1970s (287). In the present context, this similarity should not be taken to suggest that Black Consciousness was simply a mirror image of the language of the state: it had its own sources, notably Frantz Fanon and some of the writings of African Americans such as Stokely Carmichael and Malcolm X, but Black Consciousness did contribute to the climate of Manichaeanism which was characteristic of the period and to which the novel clearly responds.

5. Paul Rich's discussion of the "decline of civilization" in *Barbarians* and *July's People* touches on similar ground, although Rich chooses not to see Coetzee's novel as parodic.

6. Both Teresa Dovey ("Allegory vs. Allegory") and Wade ("The Allegorical Text and History") have provided interesting discussions of some of the allegorizing tendencies in *Barbarians* by relating them to Walter Benjamin's *Origin of German Tragic Drama*, especially the famous dictum "Allegories are, in the realm of thoughts, what ruins are, in the realm of things." Although both arguments stress indeterminacy, the point I wish to emphasize is that the novel continually frustrates the allegorizing impulse, disallowing even inconclusive or qualified meanings to emerge. For Wade, the novel's allegorizing is about historical catastrophe and systemic crisis in South Africa; for Dovey, it dispenses lessons about textuality. Both readings are valid to a point, but against them I argue that inconclusive allegorical markers are given in the novel principally in order to present the Magistrate as being unable to transform them into the stable signifiers of historical discourse.

7. I am grateful to Nicholas Visser for this point.

8. In "Into the Dark Chamber" Coetzee writes about the moral problem of fictionalizing torture without reproducing the original relations of torturer to victim.

9. René Girard's theory of mimetic desire is also applicable to the Magistrate's actions regarding the girl. The Magistrate imitates the desire of Joll, expressed in torture. The point is worth making because Coetzee applies Girardian thinking in an analysis of the "triangular structure of desire" in advertising, in an essay published in 1980 (the same year as *Barbarians*). However, the theory can offer only a partial description of the relationship; the Magistrate's *awakening* to the fact that his desire is diabolically complicit with Joll's suggests that we should examine his actions in other ways as well.

10. Teresa Dovey's analysis of *Barbarians* examines the novel as a parody showing the limits of liberal novelistic discourse, especially its unwillingness to recognize its constitution within language (*Novels of J. M. Coetzee*, chap. 4).

NOTES TO CHAPTER FOUR

1. Future projection in contemporary South African fiction goes back at least as far as Karel Schoeman's *Na Die Geliefde Land* (later translated as *Promised*

Land), first published in 1972. However, in the 1980s the trend culminated in Mongane Serote's *To Every Birth Its Blood* (1981), Gordimer's *July's People* (1981) and *A Sport of Nature* (1987), and, of course, *Michael K*. Several critics have attended to the anticipation of revolution in contemporary South African fiction, on the basis of a selection of these novels. See Bernth Lindfors, "Coming to Terms"; Margaret Lenta, "Fictions of the Future"; Sheila Roberts, "Questionable Future"; Stephen Clingman, "Revolution and Reality"; Nicholas Visser, "Beyond the Interregnum."

2. One might apply to this opposition the notion of the "exaggerated Oedipus" with which Deleuze and Guattari describe Kafka's politics (see note 3). The exaggerated Oedipus represents a broadly political application of the Freudian family romance.

3. Michael Marais, in "Languages of Power," offers an insightful and more complete analysis of this pattern. It is worth noting that the metaphor of parasitism represents a considerable extension of Coetzee's earlier figure of unequal power relations, the Hegelian master-slave dialectic.

4. See Marjanne F. Goozé, "Texts, Textuality, and Silence." Dovey's commentary on the allusions to Kafka is illuminating (*Novels of J. M. Coetzee* 298–304). I share with her an interest in Coetzee's concern with the fate of narration itself, as this concern is defined in relation to the implicitly self-referential aspect of works such as *The Castle* and "The Hunger Artist." In Dovey's argument, this is a step toward the larger allegory of the unrepresentable status of unconscious desire; I choose to keep within the more limited focus of the survival of the subject of enunciation within a discursively policed culture.

5. Coetzee cannot be taken to exemplify all the features of "minor literature" as defined by Deleuze and Guattari. Although Coetzee does "deterritorialize" the colonial language in sometimes dramatic ways (as in *Barbarians*), and although his fiction is political in the sense that it takes stock of its historical location, he does not represent a "collective" form of enunciation, as Kafka does in this description (Deleuze and Guattari 16–27).

6. See the description in "Richard Steele's Narrative of Selkirk" (reprinted in Rogers 162).

7. An adequate survey of this vast tradition is impossible here. Martin Green notes that by 1895 there had been 115 revisions, 277 imitations (the Robinsonades), 110 translations, and 196 English editions (92). I am relying on Catherine Glenn-Lauga's discussion of *Foe* in relation to the French tradition, which Coetzee seems to know (J. Giraudoux precedes Coetzee in having a female protagonist, called Suzanne, enter the story). Glenn-Lauga's analysis encompasses Giraudoux, *Suzanne et la Pacifique*; Saint-John Perse, *Images à Crusoé*; Michel Tournier, *Vendredi ou les limbes du pacifique*; Valéry, "Robinson" in *Histoires brisées*; and Jules Verne, *L'île mystérieuse*.

8. Coetzee's concerns bear comparison with Spivak's remarks on the problem of representing subaltern consciousness in "Subaltern Studies" (202–7). Representation, Spivak argues, should be seen as the production of a "subaltern subject-effect" that is articulated through "politics, ideology, economics, history, sexuality, language, and so on." In "Theory in the Margin," however,

Spivak suggests that such work must also be regarded as centered, that is, as subject to the power to withhold on the part of the "wholly Other." Benita Parry challenges some of the excesses of colonial discourse analysis by arguing that the emphasis on the nonrepresentability of the subaltern could serve to reproduce cultural imperialism's silencing of the colonized ("Problems in Current Theories of Colonial Discourse"). Spivak replies to this objection by arguing that even well-intentioned representations of the Other are subject to Friday's power to withhold.

NOTES TO CHAPTER FIVE

1. Coetzee is referring to Francis Fukuyama, "The End of History?"

Works Cited

Alexander, Neville. "A Plea for a New World." Rev. of *Foe*, by J. M. Coetzee. *Die Suid-Afrikaan* 10 (Spring 1987): 38.

Armbruster, Frank E., Raymond D. Gastil, Herman Kahn, William Pfaff, and Edmund Stillman. *Can We Win in Vietnam? The American Dilemma*. London: Pall Mall Press, 1968.

Attridge, Derek. "Oppressive Silence: J. M. Coetzee's *Foe* and the Politics of the Canon." *Decolonizing the Tradition: New Views of Twentieth-Century "British" Literary Canons*. Ed. Karen Lawrence. Urbana: U of Illinois P, 1992. 212–38.

Attwell, David. "The Problem of History in the Fiction of J. M. Coetzee." *Rendering Things Visible: Essays on South African Literary Culture*. Ed. Martin Trump. Johannesburg: Ravan, 1990. 94–133. Rpt. *Poetics Today* 11.3 (Fall 1990): 579–615.

————— Rev. of *The Novels of J. M. Coetzee: Lacanian Allegories*, by Teresa Dovey. *Research in African Literatures* 20 (1989): 515–19.

Barthes, Roland. "Introduction to the Structural Analysis of Narratives." *Image-Music-Text*. 1966. London: Fontana, 1977. 79–124.

————— *S/Z*. Trans. Richard Miller. New York: Hill and Wang, 1974.

Beckett, Samuel. *Three Novels by Samuel Beckett: Molloy, Malone Dies, and The Unnamable*. New York: Grove, 1965.

————— *Waiting for Godot*. 1956. London and Boston: Faber and Faber, 1978.

Brink, Carel Frederik, and Johannes Tobias Rhenius. *The Journals of Brink and Rhenius, being The Journal of Carel Frederik Brink of the Journey into Great Namaqualand (1761–2) made by Captain Hendrik Hop and The Journal of Ensign Johannes Tobias Rhenius (1724)*. Ed. and trans. E. E. Mossop. Cape Town: Van Riebeeck Society, 1947.

Carusi, Annamaria. *"Foe*: The Narrative and Power." *Journal of Literary Studies* 5.2 (June 1989): 134–44.

———— "Post, Post, Post; or, Where Is South African Literature in All This?" *Ariel* 20.4 (Oct. 1989): 79–95.

Castillo, Debra A. "Coetzee's *Dusklands*: The Mythic *Punctum.*" *PMLA* 105 (1990): 1108–22.

———— "The Composition of the Self in Coetzee's *Waiting for the Barbarians.*" *Critique: Studies in Modern Fiction* 27.2 (1986): 78–90.

Cavafy, C. P. *Collected Poems.* Ed. George Savidis. Trans. Edmund Keeley and Philip Sherrard. Princeton: Princeton UP, 1975.

Chapman, Michael. "The Writing of Politics and the Politics of Writing: On Reading Dovey on Reading Lacan on Reading Coetzee on Reading . . . (?)." Rev. of *The Novels of J. M. Coetzee: Lacanian Allegories*, by Teresa Dovey. *Journal of Literary Studies* 4 (1988): 327–41

Chomsky, Noam. *American Power and the New Mandarins.* Harmondsworth: Penguin, 1969.

———— *Aspects of the Theory of Syntax.* Cambridge: MIT Press, 1965.

———— *The Backroom Boys.* London: Fontana/Collins, 1973.

Clingman, Stephen. *The Novels of Nadine Gordimer: History from the Inside.* London: Allen and Unwin, 1986.

———— "Revolution and Reality: South African Fiction in the 1980s." *Rendering Things Visible: Essays on South African Literary Culture.* Ed. Martin Trump. Johannesburg: Ravan, 1990. 41–60.

Coetzee, J. M. "Achterberg's 'Ballade van de gasfitter': The Mystery of I and You." *PMLA* (1977): 285–96.

———— "The Agentless Sentence as Rhetorical Device." *Language and Style* 13.1 (1980): 26–34.

———— *Age of Iron.* London: Secker and Warburg, 1990.

———— "Alex La Guma and the Responsibilities of the South African Writer." *New African Literature and the Arts*, vol. 3. Ed. Joseph Okpaku. New York: Third World, 1973. 116–24.

———— "Apartheid: La littérature mutilée." *Le nouvel observateur* 8–14 May 1987: 57–58.

———— "Author on History's Cutting Edge. South Africa's J. M. Coetzee: Visions of Doomed Heroics." Interview. *Washington Post* 27 Nov. 1990: C1, C4.

———— "Confession and Double Thoughts: Tolstoy, Rousseau, and Dostoevsky." *Comparative Literature* 37.3 (1985): 193–232.

———— *Doubling the Point: Essays and Interviews.* Ed. David Attwell. Cambridge: Harvard UP, 1992.

———— *Dusklands.* Johannesburg: Ravan, 1974.

———— "The English Fiction of Samuel Beckett: An Essay in Stylistic Analysis." Diss. U of Texas at Austin, 1969.

———— "The First Sentence of Yvonne Burgess's *The Strike.*" *English in Africa* 3.1 (1976): 47–48.

———— *Foe.* Johannesburg: Ravan, 1986.

———— "Grubbing for the Ideological Implications: A Clash (More or Less) with J. M. Coetzee." Interview. A. Thorold and R. Wicksteed. *Sjambok* (U of Cape Town), n.d.

———— "How I Learned about America—and Africa—in Texas." *New York Times Book Review* 15 Apr. 1984: 9.

———— "Interview de J. M. Coetzee." J. Sévry. Photocopy. Société des anglicistes de l'enseignement superieur. Colloque de Brest, 9–11 May 1985. Ed. Jean Sevry. Montpellier: Université Paul Valéry, 1985.

———— *In the Heart of the Country.* Johannesburg: Ravan, 1978.

———— "Into the Dark Chamber: The Novelist and South Africa." *New York Times Book Review* 12 Jan. 1986: 13, 35.

———— *Life and Times of Michael K.* Johannesburg: Ravan, 1983.

———— "Man's Fate in the Novels of Alex La Guma." *Studies in Black Literature* 4.4 (Winter 1974): 16–23. [The bibliographical information on the original journal is in error; it should be 5.1, Spring 1974.]

———— "Nabokov's *Pale Fire* and the Primacy of Art." *UCT Studies in English* 5 (1974): 1–7.

———— "Newton and the Ideal of a Transparent Scientific Language." *Journal of Literary Semantics* 11.1 (1982): 3–13.

———— "A Note on Writing." *Momentum: On Recent South African Writing.* Ed. M. J. Daymond, J. U. Jacobs, and Margaret Lenta. Pietermaritzburg: U of Natal P, 1984. 11–13.

———— "The Novel Today." *Upstream* 6.1 (Summer 1988): 2–5.

———— "The Rhetoric of the Passive in English." *Linguistics* 18.3–4 (1980): 199–221.

———— "Speaking: J. M. Coetzee." Interview. Stephen Watson. *Speak* 1.3 (1978): 23–24.

———— "Time, Tense, and Aspect in Kafka's 'The Burrow.'" *Modern Language Notes* 96.3 (1981): 556–79.

———— "Too Late for Politics?" Interview. *Buffalo Arts Review* 5.1 (Spring 1987): 6.

———— "Two Interviews with J. M. Coetzee, 1983 and 1987." Tony Morphet. *Triquarterly* 69 (1987): 454–64. (First interview rpt. from *Social Dynamics* 10.1 [1984]: 62–65.)

———— *Waiting for the Barbarians.* Johannesburg: Ravan, 1981.

———— *White Writing: On the Culture of Letters in South Africa.* Johannesburg: Radix (in association with Yale UP), 1988.

Coetzee, N. A. *Die Stamouers Coetzee en Nageslagte: Herdenkingsuitgawe, 300 Jaar in Suid-Afrika.* Pretoria: N. A. Coetzee, 1979.

Coser, Rose Laub, ed. *The Family: Its Structures and Functions.* New York: St. Martin's, 1974.

Defoe, Daniel. *The life and strange adventures of Robinson Crusoe of York, mariner: who lived eight and twenty years all alone in an un-inhabited island on the coast of America, near the mouth of the great river Oroonoque, having been cast on shore by shipwreck wherein all the men perished but himself.* 1719. Ed. J. Donald Crowley. London and New York: Oxford UP, 1972.

————— *Roxana: The Fortunate Mistress.* 1724. London: Simpkin Marshall, 1933.

de Kok, Ingrid, and Karen Press, eds. *Spring Is Rebellious: Arguments about Cultural Freedom by Albie Sachs and Respondents.* Cape Town: Buchu, 1990.

Deleuze, Gilles, and Guattari, Félix. *Kafka: Towards a Minor Literature.* 1975. Trans. Dana Polan. Minneapolis: U of Minnesota P, 1986.

de Saussure, Ferdinand. *Course in General Linguistics.* 1959. Ed. Charles Bally and Albert Sechehaye, in collaboration with Albert Riedlinger. Trans. Wade Baskin. New York: McGraw, 1966.

Dodd, Josephine. "Naming and Framing: Naturalization and Colonization in J. M. Coetzee's *In the Heart of the Country.*" *World Literature Written in English* 27.2 (1987): 153–61.

Dottin, Paul. *The Life and Strange Adventures of Daniel Defoe.* Trans. Louise Ragan. New York: Macaulay, 1929.

Douglas, Mary. *Purity and Danger: An Analysis of the Concepts of Pollution and Taboo.* 1966. London: Routledge, 1985.

Dovey, Teresa. "Allegory vs. Allegory: The Divorce of Different Modes of Allegorical Perception in Coetzee's *Waiting for the Barbarians.*" *Journal of Literary Studies* 4.2 (1988): 133–43.

————— "Coetzee and His Critics: The Case of *Dusklands.*" *English in Africa* 14.2 (Oct. 1987): 15–30.

————— "Introduction." Goddard and Read, *J. M. Coetzee* 1–14.

————— *The Novels of J. M. Coetzee: Lacanian Allegories.* Johannesburg: Ad Donker, 1988.

During, Simon. "Postmodernism or Postcolonialism?" *Landfall* 39.3 (Sept. 1985): 366–80.

Eckstein, Barbara. "The Body, the Word, and the State: J. M. Coetzee's *Waiting for the Barbarians.*" *Novel* 22.2 (1989): 175–98.

Flaubert, Gustave. *Bouvard et Pécuchet.* Paris: Editions Gallimard, 1950.

Foucault, Michel. *The Archeology of Knowledge.* Trans. A. M. Sheridan Smith. London: Tavistock, 1972.

————— *Discipline and Punish: The Birth of the Prison.* 1975. Trans. Alan Sheridan. New York: Vintage-Random, 1979.

————— "Language to Infinity." *Language, Counter-Memory, Practice: Selected Essays and Interviews.* Ed. Donald f. Bouchard. Trans. Donald f. Bouchard and Sherry Simon. Ithaca: Cornell UP, 1977. 53–67.

————— *Power/Knowledge: Selected Interviews and Other Writings, 1972–1977.* Ed. Colin Gordon. Trans. Colin Gordon, Leo Marshall, John Mepham, and Kate Soper. New York: Pantheon-Random, 1980.

Freud, Sigmund. *Totem and Taboo. The Basic Writings of Sigmund Freud.* Ed. and trans. A. A. Brill. New York: Random, 1938.

Fukuyama, Francis. "The End of History?" *National Interest* 16 (Summer 1989): 3–18.

Furet, François. "Civilization and Barbarism in Gibbon's History." *The Workshop of History.* Chicago: U of Chicago P, 1982. 140–49.

Galan, F. W. *Historic Structures: The Prague School Project, 1928–1948.* Austin: U of Texas P, 1985.

Gallagher, Susan Van Zanten. "Torture and the Novel: J. M. Coetzee's *Waiting for the Barbarians.*" *Contemporary Literature* 29.2 (1988): 277–85.

Gibbon, Edward. *The Portable Gibbon: The Decline and Fall of the Roman Empire.* Ed. Dero A. Saunders. New York: Viking, 1952.

Girard, René. *Deceit, Desire, and the Novel: Self and Other in Literary Structure.* 1961. Trans. Yvonne Freccero. Baltimore: Johns Hopkins UP, 1965.

Glenn-Lauga, Catherine. "The Hearerly Text: Sea Shells on the Sea Shore." *Journal of Literary Studies* 5.2 (June 1989): 194–214.

Goddard, Kevin, and John Read, eds. *J. M. Coetzee: A Bibliography.* National English Literary Museum Bibliographic Series 3. Grahamstown, S.A.: NELM, 1990.

Goozé, Marjanne f. "Texts, Textuality, and Silence in Franz Kafka's *Das Schloß.*" *Modern Language Notes* 98 (1983): 337–50.

Gordimer, Nadine. *Burger's Daughter.* New York: Viking, 1979.

——— "The Essential Gesture." Gordimer, *Essential Gesture* 285–300.

——— *The Essential Gesture: Writing, Politics, and Places.* 1988. Ed. Stephen Clingman. London: Penguin, 1989.

——— "The Idea of Gardening." *New York Review of Books* 2 Feb. 1984: 3, 6.

——— *July's People.* 1981. Harmondsworth: Penguin, 1982.

——— "Living in the Interregnum." Gordimer, *Essential Gesture* 261–84.

——— *A Sport of Nature.* Cape Town: David Philip, 1987.

Gräbe, Ina. "Postmodern Narrative Strategies in *Foe.*" *Journal of Literary Studies* 5.2 (June 1989): 145–82.

Gramsci, Antonio. *Selections from the Prison Notebooks.* Ed. and trans. Quinton Hoare and Geoffrey Nowell Smith. New York: International Publishers, 1971.

Gray, Stephen. *Southern African Literature: An Introduction.* New York: Harper, 1979.

Green, Martin. *Dreams of Adventure and Deeds of Empire.* New York: Basic Books, 1979.

Haggard, Rider H. *King Solomon's Mines.* 1885. London and Glasgow: Blackie, 1961.

Haluska, Jan Charles. "Master and Slave in the First Four Novels of J. M. Coetzee." Diss. U of Tennessee, Knoxville, 1987.

Hegel, G. W. f. *The Phenomenology of Mind.* 1910. Trans. J. B. Bailie. London: Allen and Unwin, 1977.

Heraclitus. *Fragments.* Text and translation with commentary by T. M. Robinson. Toronto: U of Toronto P, 1987.

Ho Chi Minh. *Selected Writings: 1920–1969.* Hanoi: Foreign Languages Publishing House, 1977.

Hutcheon, Linda. *Narcissistic Narrative: The Metafictional Paradox.* New York: Methuen, 1980.

——— *A Poetics of Postmodernism: History, Theory, Fiction.* New York and London: Routledge, 1988.

———— *The Politics of Postmodernism*. London and New York: Routledge, 1989.

———— *A Theory of Parody: The Teachings of Twentieth Century Art Forms*. New York and London: Methuen, 1985.

Jameson, Fredric. "Modernism and Its Repressed; or, Robbe-Grillet as Anticolonialist." *The Ideologies of Theory: Essays 1971–1986*. Vol. 1, *Situations of Theory*. London: Routledge, 1988. 167–80.

———— "Periodizing the 60s." *The Ideologies of Theory: Essays 1971–1986*. Vol. 2, *Syntax of History*. London: Routledge, 1988. 178–208.

———— *The Political Unconscious: Narrative as a Socially Symbolic Act*. London: Methuen, 1981.

———— "Postmodernism; or, The Cultural Logic of Late Capitalism." *New Left Review* 146 (July–Aug. 1984): 53–92.

———— *The Prison-House of Language: A Critical Account of Structuralism and Russian Formalism*. Princeton: Princeton UP, 1972.

Jefferson, Ann. *The Nouveau Roman and the Poetics of Fiction*. Cambridge: Cambridge UP, 1980.

Jolly, Rosemary Jane. "Territorial Metaphor in Coetzee's *Waiting for the Barbarians*." *Ariel* 20.2 (Apr. 1990): 69–79.

Kafka, Franz. *Selected Short Stories*. 1932. Trans. Willa and Edwin Muir. New York: Random, 1952.

Kenner, Hugh. *Flaubert, Joyce, and Beckett: The Stoic Comedians*. London: W. H. Allen, 1964.

———— *Samuel Beckett: A Critical Study*. 1961. Berkeley and Los Angeles: U of California P, 1968.

Kermode, John Frank. *The Sense of an Ending: Studies in the Theory of Fiction*. New York: Oxford UP, 1967.

Kirkwood, Mike. "The Colonizer: A Critique of the English South African Culture Theory." *Poetry South Africa: Selected Papers from Poetry '74*. Ed. Peter Wilhelm and James A. Polley. Cape Town: Ad Donker, 1976. 102–33.

Knox-Shaw, Peter. "*Dusklands*: A Metaphysics of Violence." *Contrast* 14.1 (1982): 26–38.

Kohler, Peter. "Freeburghers, the Nama, and the Politics of the Frontier Tradition: An Analysis of Social Relations in the Second Narrative of J. M. Coetzee's *Dusklands*. Towards an Historiography of South African Literature." The Making of Class. History workshop, U of the Witwatersrand, 1987.

Lazarus, Neil. "Modernism and Modernity: T. W. Adorno and Contemporary White South African Literature." *Cultural Critique* 5 (Winter 1987): 131–55.

Lenta, Margaret. "Fictions of the Future." *English Academy Review* 5 (1988): 133–45.

Lindfors, Bernth. "Coming to Terms with the Apocalypse: Recent South African Fiction." *A Sense of Place: Essays in Post-Colonial Literatures*. Ed. Britta Olinder. Göteborg: Göteborg UP, 1984. 196–203.

Lukács, Georg. *History and Class Consciousness: Studies in Marxist Dialectics*. Trans. Rodney Livingstone. London: Merlin, 1971.

Lyotard, Jean-François. *The Postmodern Condition: A Report on Knowledge.* 1979. Trans. Geoff Bennington and Brian Massumi. Minneapolis: U of Minnesota P, 1984.

Malinowski, Bronislaw. "Parenthood, the Basis of Social Structure." Coser, *The Family* 51–63.

Marais, Michael. "Languages of Power: A Story of Reading *Michael K*/Michael K." *English in Africa* 16.2 (Oct. 1989): 31–48.

Marcuse, Herbert. *One Dimensional Man.* 1964. London: Abacus, 1974.

Marks, Shula. "The Historiography of South Africa: Recent Developments." *African Historiographies: What History for Which Africa?* Ed. Bogumil Jewsiewicki and David Newbury. Beverly Hills: Sage, 1986. 165–76.

Martin, Richard G. "Narrative, History, Ideology: A Study of *Waiting for the Barbarians* and *Burger's Daughter*." *Ariel* 17.3 (1986): 3–21.

Moodie, Donald. *The Record, Or a Series of Official Papers Relative to the Condition and Treatment of the Native Tribes of South Africa.* Trans. and ed. Donald Moodie. Cape Town and Amsterdam: A. A. Balkema, 1959.

Morphet, Tony. "Brushing History Against the Grain: Oppositional Discourse in South Africa." (Richard Turner Memorial Lecture, U of Natal, Durban, 27 Sept. 1990.) *Theoria* 76 (Oct. 1990): 89–99.

—— "Introduction." *The Eye of the Needle*, by Richard Turner. 1972. Johannesburg: Ravan, 1980.

Morris, Mike. "Social History and the Transition to Capitalism in South Africa." *Africa Perpective* Dec. 1987: 7–24.

Nabokov, Vladimir. *Pale Fire.* 1962. Harmondsworth: Penguin, 1973.

Ndebele, Njabulo. "Actors and Interpreters: Popular Culture and Progressive Formalism." Sol Plaatje Memorial Lecture, U of Bophuthatswana, 14 Sept. 1984.

—— "The Rediscovery of the Ordinary: Some New Writings in South Africa." *Journal of Southern African Studies* 12.2 (Apr. 1986): 143–57.

—— "Turkish Tales, and Some Thoughts on S. A. Fiction." Rev. of *Anatolian Tales*, by Yasher Kemal. *Staffrider* 6.1 (1984): 24–25, 42–48.

Nkosi, Lewis. "Fiction by Black South Africans: Richard Rive, Bloke Modisane, Ezekiel Mphahlele, Alex La Guma." *Introduction to African Literature: An Anthology of Critical Writing.* Ed. Ulli Beier. London: Longman, 1979. 221–27.

—— "Resistance and the Crisis of Representation." Second Conference on South African Literature, Evangelische Akademie, Bad Boll, West Germany, 11–13 Dec. 1987. *Dokumente Texte und Tendenzen: South African Literature: From Popular Culture to the Written Artefact.* 1988. 39–51.

Norval, A. J. "The Construction of Social Identities and Political Frontiers in Apartheid Discourse (1958–1978)." Diss. U of Essex, 1986.

O'Connell, L. C. "Traditional Allegory and Its Postmodern Use in the Novels of J. M. Coetzee." Diss. Potchefstroomse Universiteit vir Christelike Hoër Onderwys, 1988.

Olsen, Lance. "The Presence of Absence: Coetzee's *Waiting for the Barbarians*." *Ariel* 16.2 (1985): 47–56.

Parry, Benita. "Problems in Current Theories of Colonial Discourse." *Oxford Literary Review* 9.1–2 (1987): 27–58.

Paton, Alan. *Cry, the Beloved Country*. New York: Scribner's, 1948.

Penner, Dick. *Countries of the Mind: The Fiction of J. M. Coetzee*. Westport, CT: Greenwood, 1989.

Posel, Deborah. "Language, Legitimation, and Control: The South African State after 1978." *Social Dynamics* 10.1 (1984): 1–16.

Press, Karen. *Towards a Revolutionary Artistic Practice in South Africa*. Diss. Centre for African Studies, U of Cape Town, Jan. 1988.

Rich, Paul. "Apartheid and the Decline of the Civilization Idea: An Essay on Nadine Gordimer's *July's People* and J. M. Coetzee's *Waiting for the Barbarians*." *Research in African Literatures* 15.3 (Fall 1984): 365–93.

Richetti, John J. *Daniel Defoe*. Boston: Twayne, 1987.

Ricoeur, Paul. "The Narrative Function." *Hermeneutics and the Human Sciences: Essays on Language, Action, and Interpretation*. Trans. and ed. John B. Thompson. Cambridge: Cambridge UP, 1981. 274–96.

Rive, Richard. "Introduction." Schreiner, *Story of an African Farm* 7–20.

Roberts, Sheila. "A Questionable Future: The Vision of Revolution in White South African Writing." *Journal of Contemporary African Studies* 4.1–2 (Oct. 1984–Apr. 1985): 215–23.

Rogers, Pat. *Robinson Crusoe*. London: Allen and Unwin, 1979.

Sachs, Albie. "Preparing Ourselves for Freedom." De Kok and Press 19–29.

Said, Edward W. *Orientalism*. 1978. New York: Vintage-Random, 1979.

—— "Representing the Colonized: Anthropology's Interlocutors." *Critical Inquiry* 15.3 (Spring 1989): 205–25.

—— "The World, the Text, and the Critic." *The World, the Text, and the Critic*. Cambridge: Harvard UP, 1983. 31–53.

Schlebusch Commission. *Fourth Interim Report of the Commission of Inquiry into Certain Organizations*. Pretoria: Government Printer, 1974.

Schoeman, Karel. *Na Die Geliefde Land*. Cape Town and Pretoria: Human and Rousseau, 1972.

Scholes, Robert. *Fabulation and Metafiction*. Urbana: U of Illinois P, 1979.

Schreiner, Olive. *The Story of an African Farm*. 1883. Johannesburg: Ad Donker, 1975.

—— *Trooper Peter Halket of Mashonaland*. London: T. Fisher Unwin, 1897.

Sepamla, Sipho. *A Ride on the Whirlwind: A Novel of Soweto*. Johannesburg: Ad Donker, 1981.

Serote, Mongane. *To Every Birth Its Blood*. Johannesburg: Ravan, 1981.

Siegle, Robert. *The Politics of Reflexivity: Narrative and the Constitutive Poetics of Culture*. Baltimore: Johns Hopkins UP, 1986.

Skalnik, Peter. "Tribe as Colonial Category." *South African Keywords*. Ed. Emile Boonzaaier and John Sharp. Cape Town: David Philip, 1983. 68–78.

Slater, Philip. "Social Limitations on Libidinal Withdrawal." Coser, *The Family* 111–33.

Slemon, Stephen. "Modernism's Last Post." *Ariel* 20.4 (Oct. 1989): 3–17.

—— "Post-Colonial Allegory and the Transformation of History." *Journal of Commonwealth Literature* 13.1 (1988): 157–68.

South African Institute of Race Relations. *Survey of Race Relations in South Africa: 1980.* Ed. Loraine Gordon. Johannesburg: South African Institute of Race Relations, 1981.

Spengler, Oswald. *The Decline of the West: Form and Actuality.* Trans. Charles Francis Atkinson. 2 vols. London: Allen and Unwin, 1926.

Spivak, Gayatri Chakravorty. "Subaltern Studies: Deconstructing Historiography." *In Other Worlds: Essays in Cultural Politics.* New York and London: Methuen, 1987. 197–221.

—— "Theory in the Margin: Coetzee's *Foe* Reading Defoe's *Crusoe/Roxana.*" *English in Africa* 17.2 (Oct. 1990). 1 23. Rpt. *Consequences of Theory. Selected Papers from the English Institute, 1987–1988.* Ed. Jonathan Arac and Barbara Johnson. Baltimore: Johns Hopkins UP, 1990.

—— "Three Women's Texts and a Critique of Imperialism." *Critical Inquiry* 12.1 (Autumn 1985): 243–61.

—— "Translator's Preface." *Of Grammatology,* by Jacques Derrida. 1967. Baltimore: Johns Hopkins UP, 1976. ix–lxxxvii.

Stadler, Alf. *The Political Economy of Modern South Africa.* Cape Town: David Philip, 1987.

Study Project on Christianity in Apartheid Society (SPRO-CAS). *South Africa's Political Alternatives.* Report of the Political Commission. Johannesburg: Ravan, 1973.

Tiffin, Helen. "Post-Colonialism, Post-Modernism, and the Rehabilitation of Post-Colonial History." *Journal of Commonwealth Literature* 13.1 (1988): 169–81.

—— "Post-Colonial Literatures and Counter-Discourse." *Kunapipi* 9.3 (1987): 17–34.

Turner, Richard. *The Eye of the Needle.* 1972. Johannesburg: Ravan, 1980.

—— "Marcuse: The Power of Negative Thinking." *Radical* 1 (1970): 29–33.

Vaughan, Michael. "Literature and Politics: Currents in South African Writing in the Seventies." *Journal of Southern African Studies* 9.1 (Oct. 1982): 118–38.

Visser, Nicholas. "Beyond the Interregnum: A Note on the Ending of *July's People.*" *Rendering Things Visible: Essays on South African Literary Culture.* Ed. Martin Trump. Johannesburg: Ravan, 1990. 61–67.

Wade, Jean-Phillipe. "The Allegorical Text and History: J. M. Coetzee's *Waiting for the Barbarians.*" *Journal of Literary Studies* 6.4 (Dec. 1990): 275–88.

Watson, Stephen. "Colonialism and the Novels of J. M. Coetzee." *Research in African Literatures* 17.3 (Fall 1986): 370–92.

Waugh, Patricia. *Metafiction: The Theory and Practice of Self-Conscious Fiction.* London: Methuen, 1984.

White, Hayden. *Metahistory: The Historical Imagination in Nineteenth-Century Europe.* Baltimore: Johns Hopkins UP, 1973.

Wikar, Hendrik Jacob, Jacobus Jansz Coetsé, and Willem van Reenen. *The Journal of Hendrik Jacob Wikar (1779), and The Journals of Jacobus Coetsé Jansz and Willem van Reenen.* Trans. A. W. van der Horst. Ed. E. E. Mossop. Cape Town: Van Riebeeck Society, 1935.

Williams, P. A. "The Divided Self in the Novels of J. M. Coetzee." Diss. U of Natal, Durban, 1985.

Wright, Derek. "Fiction as Foe: The Novels of J. M. Coetzee." *International Fiction Review* 16.2 (1989): 112–18.

Wright, Thomas. *The Life of Daniel Defoe.* London: C. J. Forncombe and Sons, 1931.

Z. N. "Much Ado about Nobody." Rev. of *Life and Times of Michael K*, by J. M. Coetzee. *African Communist* 97 (1984): 101–3.

Index

Lightning Source UK Ltd.
Milton Keynes UK
UKHW012132201221
395985UK00002B/135